OECD Public Governance Reviews

Open Government Scan of Lebanon

Please cite this publication as:
OECD (2020), *Open Government Scan of Lebanon*, OECD Public Governance Reviews, OECD Publishing, Paris, *https://doi.org/10.1787/d7cce8c0-en*.

ISBN 978-92-64-36598-8 (print)
ISBN 978-92-64-41846-2 (pdf)

OECD Public Governance Reviews
ISSN 2219-0406 (print)
ISSN 2219-0414 (online)

Photo credits: Cover © Kertu/Shutterstock.com.

Corrigenda to publications may be found on line at: *www.oecd.org/about/publishing/corrigenda.htm*.

Foreword

Around the world, governments are facing increasingly complex challenges, including persistently low levels of public trust, rising economic and financial instability, and social fragmentation and polarisation. Meanwhile, citizens are becoming more vocal, particularly given the amplifying effect of digital technologies, and their expectations are growing for a more transparent and accountable public sector and better public services. These issues are especially relevant in Lebanon, where regional turmoil, political instability and sluggish economic growth have posed considerable obstacles.

Open government represents a changed understanding of the role of the state in a modern society that aligns with an underlying shift in the policy-making context. The OECD defines it as "a culture of governance that promotes the principles of transparency, integrity, accountability and stakeholder participation in support of democracy and inclusive growth". More and more countries have begun to introduce open government reforms as a catalyst for attaining broader policy goals such as improving democracy, fostering inclusive growth and increasing trust. However, beyond the intrinsic value of open government principles, the implementation of open government strategies and initiatives can also help improve processes and outcomes across the full spectrum of public policy.

For several years, successive Lebanese governments have taken steps to establish a national open government agenda; however, the context has been challenging. In particular, large-scale demonstrations erupted in October 2019, bringing about the resignation of the government. At the same time, the country has also been weathering a severe financial crisis, which has been exacerbated by the coronavirus (Covid-19) pandemic, putting further strains on scarce human and financial resources. Most recently, the catastrophic explosion in the port of Beirut has underlined a number of public sector governance failures that must be addressed in order to rebuild trust between the citizens and the state. Although this context presents significant challenges for the new government, it also provides an opportunity and strong incentive to restore public trust through open government reforms. Accordingly, a focus on opening up the government is not only timely, but also in demand.

Against this background, the *OECD Open Government Scan of Lebanon* aims to support the government's efforts to build more transparent, participatory, and accountable institutions that can restore citizens' trust and promote inclusive growth. It analyses priority areas of reform in line with the 2017 *OECD Recommendation of the Council on Open Government* and provides concrete suggestions for further embedding the principles and practices of open government in policy-making cycles and evaluating their impacts. Ultimately, this analysis can serve as the foundation to define and pursue a whole-of-government vision for a more open government in Lebanon.

This *Open Government Scan of Lebanon* benefits from ongoing support and dialogue with successive Lebanese governments and the Office of the Minister of State for Administrative Reform (OMSAR), which has over the past years taken steps towards establishing a national open government agenda in Lebanon. This continuous commitment was initially affirmed by former Minister May Chidiac, who formally announced OMSAR's engagement in this process as well as the Government's intent to work towards adhering to the OECD Recommendation of the Council on Open Government and joining the Open

Government Partnership, during a high-level conference co-organised with the OECD and under the patronage of the Prime Minister in June 2019.

This commitment has been re-affirmed at the beginning of 2020 by Minister Demianos Kattar, who subsequently expressed Lebanon's commitment to continue its joint work with the OECD in pursuit of an open government agenda for a more transparent, participatory, responsive, and trustworthy public administration. Building on these steps, the findings of this analysis have benefitted from the extensive review by OMSAR and from discussions with several representatives of relevant Lebanese institutions and civil society organisations as well as international organisations active in the promotion of good governance reforms Lebanon (i.e. OGP, UNDP, World Bank) and peer reviewers from Canada and Italy.

The data collection for this report and its drafting were finalised before the explosion in the port of Beirut and the ensuing government crisis. However, Lebanese public institutions had the opportunity to review its findings during the month of August 2020 and confirmed the validity of its recommendations. The OECD is currently working with OMSAR to develop an action plan to implement them.

Acknowledgements

The "Open Government Scan of Lebanon" was prepared by the OECD Directorate for Public Governance (GOV), under the leadership of its Acting Director, Janos Bertok.

The study was produced by GOV's Open and Innovative Government Division (OIG), under the supervision of Alessandro Bellantoni, Acting Head of the OIG Division and Head of the Open Government Unit.

The report was drafted by Alessandro Bellantoni, Katharina Zuegel and Claudia Chwalisz, with contributions from Carlotta Alfonsi, Karine Badr, Michael Jelenic and João Vasconselos.

This project would not have been possible without the support of the Office of the Minister of State for Administrative Reform (OMSAR) of Lebanon, and benefited greatly from the assistance of Nasser Israoui, Natacha Sarkis and May Baaklini. The OECD wishes to acknowledge the co-operation and support of the current Minister of State for Administrative Reform, Demyanos Kattar, as well as the former Minister of State for Administrative Reform, May Chidiac, in addition to the important contributions provided by the many stakeholders from the public and private sector, as well as the parliament and non-governmental organisations, during the peer review mission conducted between 17 and 19 September 2019.[1] In this regard, the OECD wishes to thank peers from Canada and Italy, namely Sarah MacLeod (Office of the Chief Information Officer, Treasury Board of Canada Secretariat) and Marco Marrazza (Presidency of Council of Ministers, Department for Public Administration).

The OECD is also grateful for the co-operation and support of Mayor Habib Moujaes, Nisrine Ataya Bou Zeid, and their colleagues in the Shweir council and administration, as well as Mayor Wissam Zaarour, Emily Bouchrouch, and their colleagues in the Byblos council and administration. The OECD would also like to thank Jacques Pongée (Brussels Parliament), Marcin Gerwin (Center for Climate Assemblies, Poland) and Dimitri Lemaire (Particitiz, Belgium) for their time and expertise devoted to the expert workshop on innovative citizen participation.

Finally, the OECD wishes to thank the Italian Ministry of Foreign Affairs and International Co-operation and the Italian Agency for Development Co-operation for the support they have provided throughout the project.

Note

[1] These include representatives from the Prime Minister's Office; Ministries of Information, Finance, Interior and Municipalities, and Justice; the Court of Audit; Central Inspection Unit; the Central Administration for Statistics; the Access to Information Technical Committee; the Technology and Information Parliamentary Committee; the Higher Education Committee; the Lebanese Oil and Gas Initiative; Gherbal Initiative; the Lebanese Transparency Association; Nahnoo; and SMEX.

Table of contents

Tables

Figures

Boxes

Follow OECD Publications on:

 http://twitter.com/OECD_Pubs

 http://www.facebook.com/OECDPublications

 http://www.linkedin.com/groups/OECD-Publications-4645871

 http://www.youtube.com/oecdilibrary

OECD Alerts http://www.oecd.org/oecddirect/

Executive Summary

Lebanon has recently expressed interest in undertaking the reforms necessary to adhere to the *OECD Recommendation on Open Government*, and in becoming eligible to join the Open Government Partnership (OGP).This *OECD Open Government Scan of Lebanon* provides, for the government's consideration, a broad range of policies and initiatives reflecting the principles of transparency, integrity, accountability and stakeholder participation.

Developing a strategy or a long-term agenda is a core step towards achieving the vision of a more open government. Chapter 2 looks at how Lebanon can bring scattered open government initiatives under one roof, strengthen their coherence and gain a stronger mandate. Chapters 3 and 4 discuss framing this vision within a sound enabling environment, including a comprehensive regulatory and legal framework and as an institutional framework that supports the effective implementation of reforms and initiatives. Given that an open government agenda or strategy needs to be continually evaluated and revised, Chapter 5 discusses how Lebanese officials can ensure that they are gathering insights and evidence to measure impact.

Subsequent chapters address how Lebanese citizens are informed, engaged and brought into the decision-making process. Chapter 6 analyses how public communication is a central function of an open government and how it can increase the impact of transparency measures by providing information to the widest possible audience. As noted in Chapter 7, Lebanon has begun integrating participatory mechanisms in some of its policy processes, which can be further expanded in the future, drawing on the valuable insights of the country's strong civil society.

The final chapters of the scan provide an view of how Lebanon can integrate the concept of an "open state" into its open government vision or strategy (Chapter 8), outline the necessary steps to attain eligibility to join the OGP (Chapter 9), and institutionalise open government practices at the decentralised level, including in the municipalities of Shweir and Jbeil (Byblos) (Chapter 10).

Summary of recommendations:

- **Towards an open government strategy:** 1) elaborate an open government action plan that includes all ongoing initiatives; 2) disseminate the plan widely to the public; and 3) develop an open government strategy for the whole of government.
- **Legal framework:** 1) update effective legal and regulatory frameworks for the digital transformation of the public sector; and 2) expand stakeholder engagement guidelines.
- **Institutional framework:** 1) formalise the role of the Office of the Minister of State for Administrative Reform (OMSAR) as the leading agency of Lebanon's open government reforms; 2) establish a committee on open government, which functions in accordance with existing government committee structures; and 3) introduce responsibilities and skills related to open government in certain job positions/descriptions.

- **Monitoring and evaluation (M&E) framework:** 1) strengthen Lebanon's M&E system by automating the process; 2) apply open government principles to the M&E system by systematically engage all relevant stakeholders and publishing results; and 3) build an M&E culture and system by developing indicators for open government initiatives.
- **Communication and information:** 1) create public communication structures across the administration; 2) consider making the official government gazette freely available to enhance transparency; 3) advance efforts to digitalise the administration and make public information readily available, in an open, easily accessible, interoperable and reusable format; and 4) consider publishing the draft budget law, the audit report, and the budget law in an open data format.
- **Participation practices and innovation:** 1) consider the establishment of an open government stakeholder network that brings together government and civil society organisations involved in the promotion of different elements of Lebanon's open government agenda; 2) adopt an inclusive and collaborative process in the design and roll-out of the planned e-participation platform for the consultation process of draft laws; and 3) strengthen stakeholder feedback and complaint mechanisms.
- **Open state:** 1) institutionalise the practice of allowing parliamentary question sessions for stakeholder participants; 2) discuss the draft budget law and the audit report in public sessions and making all relevant documents accessible; 3) include a more user-friendly design and more up-to-date information on the parliament website; 4) publish draft laws before they are discussed in parliament sessions; 5) create an informal working group of parliamentarians and administrative staff committed to open government principles; and 6) appoint an official responsible for access to information and providing training and raising awareness of parliamentary staff.
- **Lebanon's performance against the OGP minimum eligibility criteria:** 1) publish the executive budget proposal and the audit report on an annual basis; 2) publicly disclose assets alongside a system to verify the accuracy of the declarations; and 3) continue the implementation of ongoing open government reforms to improve the results of indices measuring civil liberties, civil society organisation (CSO) entry and exit, and CSO repression.
- **Open government scan of selected Lebanese municipalities:** 1) co-create an open government strategy; 2) foster exchange mechanisms with other Lebanese municipalities; 3) provide training and capacity-building activities to implement open government initiatives; 4) assign responsibilities to an individual or office for the handling of ATI requests and for stakeholder and citizen participation; 5) expand the use of public-civil partnerships for the co-delivery of public services; 6) publish the budget in an open data format at the municipal level; 7) create a citizen's guide to the budget; 8) develop a public communication strategy linked to open government; 9) publish systematic information about local projects; 10) extend communication beyond social media and develop audience insights; 11) create a Charter of Openness & Participation; 12) institutionalise stakeholder and citizen participation in planning local projects; 13) develop monitoring and evaluation guidelines for open government; 14) introduce cutting-edge citizen participation practices; 15) expand the functionality of mobile applications; 16) continue the data archive process in co-ordination with OMSAR; and 17) create a mechanism for representatives of all levels of government and OMSAR to collaborate on the national open state agenda of Lebanon.

Chapter 1. Introduction and context

The OECD framework on open government

Around the world, governments are facing increasingly complex challenges, including persistently low levels of public trust, rising economic and financial instability, and social fragmentation and polarisation. Meanwhile, citizens are becoming more vocal, particularly given the amplifying effect of digital technologies, and their expectations are growing for a more transparent and accountable public sector and better public services. These issues are especially relevant in Lebanon, where regional turmoil, political instability and sluggish economic growth have posed considerable obstacles.

Open government represents a changed understanding of the role of the state in a modern society that aligns with an underlying shift in the policy-making context. The OECD defines it as "a culture of governance that promotes the principles of transparency, integrity, accountability and stakeholder participation in support of democracy and inclusive growth" (OECD, 2017[1]). More and more countries have begun to introduce open government reforms as a catalyst for attaining broader policy goals such as improving democracy, fostering inclusive growth and increasing trust. However, beyond the intrinsic value of open government principles, the implementation of open government strategies and initiatives can also help improve processes and outcomes across the full spectrum of public policy.

A steady increase in the adoption of open government agendas and initiatives by multiple countries has served to establish this field of policy and to create a collection of international experiences and best practices. Since 2011, the Open Government Partnership (OGP) has provided a growing number of countries with a framework to undertake gradually evolving commitments to open up their governments. The OGP is a multilateral initiative that aims to secure concrete commitments from governments to promote transparency, empower citizens, fight corruption and harness new technologies to strengthen governance. It now counts over 90 members among countries and local administrations, which highlights the rapid expansion and evolution of this area of policy.

Building on the collective experiences of its members and partners, the OECD introduced the Recommendation of the Council on Open Government in 2017, the first internationally recognised legal instrument on open government. The adoption of the Recommendation followed on from more than 15 years of evidence-based analysis of open government strategies and initiatives, the OECD report, "Open Government: the Global Context and the Way Forward" (OECD, 2016[2]), as well as a successful online public consultation. The recommendation provides the substantive framework for all the work the OECD implements in this policy area and guides the work of the OECD Working Party on Open Government, which brings together OECD member and partner countries to discuss how to further advance open government and open state reforms.

Lebanon's context and approach to open government reforms

For several years, successive Lebanese governments have taken steps to establish a national open government agenda; however, the context has been challenging. In particular, large-scale demonstrations erupted in October 2019, bringing about the resignation of the government. At the same time, the country has also been weathering a severe financial crisis, which has been exacerbated by the coronavirus (Covid-19) pandemic, putting further strains on scarce human and financial resources. Most recently, the catastrophic explosion in the port of Beirut has underlined a number of public sector governance failures that must be addressed in order to rebuild trust between the citizens and the state. Although this context presents significant challenges for the new government, it also provides an opportunity and strong incentive to restore public trust through open government reforms. Accordingly, a focus on opening up the government is not only timely, but also in demand.

Even before the explosion in the port of Beirut, public discontent and demonstrations have been targeted significantly at the sectarian power-sharing agreement, which is accused of having facilitated a system of governance with low transparency and accountability. This has served to amplify the effects of political deadlocks and increase their frequency, and has discouraged citizens from engaging through traditional means in policy debates. A context where stakeholders have multiple avenues to hold their government accountable, and where they have transparent information and opportunities to contribute to public decisions, tends to improve policies and services.

A legacy of governance issues and public mismanagement is also held as a reason for the deterioration of the economic situation that has escalated into the current crisis. International partners made this connection explicit in 2018 in the context of the terms of the economic package agreed at the Economic Conference for Development through Reforms with the Private Sector (*Conférence économique pour le développement du Liban par les réformes et avec les entreprises*, CEDRE). Having grappled with one of the world's heaviest public debt burdens, exceeding 150% of gross domestic product (GDP), Lebanon defaulted on bond repayments in March 2020, in line with widespread public demand that domestic needs are prioritised to ensure the continuity of essential services (Yee, 2020[3]). Looking ahead, repairing Lebanon's credibility and restoring its access to global financial markets will rely on the successful implementation of governance reforms, in particular those addressing transparency and integrity.

Corruption is an important area for policy intervention, as recognised in the new government's Ministerial Statement of 2020.[1] For the past six years, Lebanon has scored 28 out of 100 (where 100 indicates the lowest corruption) in the Corruption Perception Index, an international measure of public sector corruption, which is below the regional average of 39 for the Middle East and North Africa (MENA) region (Lebanese Transparency Association, 2019[4]). According to the World Bank's Worldwide Governance Indicators (WGI), corruption in Lebanon has deteriorated from a score of 19.2 in 2015 to 12.0 in 2018, placing it in the bottom quartile. This is reflected in citizens' perceptions, 99% of whom believed that there was significant government corruption and 96% of whom attributed corrupt practices to political parties (Lebanese Center for Policy Studies, 2019[5]).

Against this background, the new government has placed considerable emphasis on supporting the National Anti-corruption Strategy 2020-2025, which was adopted by the Council of Ministers in May 2020. The Office of the Minister for Administrative Reform (OMSAR), has played a prominent part in this area of policy, as it chairs the Anti-corruption Technical Committee and is represented in the ministerial committee, both of which were established in 2011. The National Anti-corruption Strategy is a significant step forward and builds on the existing framework and a set of international agreements, including the UN Convention Against Corruption (UNCAC). Lebanon also announced in 2017 its intention to join the Extractive Industries Transparency Initiative (EITI), which resulted in the enactment of Law No. 84/2018 on Enhancing Transparency in the Petroleum Sector.

Alongside steps to advance anti-corruption reforms, efforts to promote open, transparent, participatory and accountable institutions in Lebanon have recently gained renewed traction. In January 2017, Lebanon introduced its Right of Access to Information Law, a landmark step towards enhancing the transparency of the public sector. Likewise, the government has worked to develop a national action plan on the implementation of the law, and is currently in the process of developing an e-portal to support the proactive disclosure of information from obligated administrations.

In parallel, the country has been measuring progress against a set of 11 measures relating to good governance that it pledged to introduce within the framework of CEDRE. These include initiatives aimed at modernising the public sector through the draft Digital Transformation Strategy and a detailed mapping exercise by OMSAR of staff and resource allocation across the entire public sector, with the objective of creating efficiencies. Lebanon has also introduced better transparency in its public finances. For instance, for several years it has been publishing the Citizens' Budget, a simplified version of the government's annual budget prepared by the Institute of Finance.

Prior to the October 2019 protests, Lebanon had expressed interest in formalising its approach to open government by taking part in international legal and institutional frameworks governing this area of policy. Specifically, it indicated its intention to undertake the reforms necessary to be able to adhere to the OECD Recommendation on Open Government and become eligible for joining the OGP.

As for all countries aspiring to become OGP members, Lebanon needs to obtain 12 points of the 16 outlined in the OGP minimum eligibility criteria in order to qualify. Currently, Lebanon meets criteria for 8 points. To obtain the additional 4 points necessary, the country needs to introduce reforms in any one area of citizen participation, budget transparency, and disclosures related to elected or senior public officials. Budget transparency presents an area in which Lebanon could make rapid gains. Accordingly, Lebanon could gain 4 missing points by publishing the executive budget proposal and audit reports for recent years. Based on the Law on Asset and Interest Declaration and the Fight against Illicit Enrichment, which was adopted on 30 September 2020, disclosures related to elected or senior public officials are required but not yet made public – the country could gain 2 points when declarations become public. Another 2 points could be gained in the citizen participation category if Lebanon improved its score on the Civil Liberty Indicator of the Economist Intelligence Unit (EIU) Democracy Index from 4.71/10 in 2019 to 7.5/10.

Box 1.1. The OECD Recommendation of the Council on Open Government

1. Develop and implement open government strategies and initiatives in collaboration with stakeholders and foster commitment from politicians, members of parliament, senior public managers and public officials.
2. Ensure the existence and implementation of the necessary open government legal and regulatory framework while establishing adequate oversight mechanisms to ensure compliance.
3. Ensure the successful operationalisation and take-up of open government strategies and initiatives.
4. Co-ordinate, through the necessary institutional mechanisms, open government strategies and initiatives – horizontally and vertically – across all levels of government to ensure that they are aligned with and contribute to all relevant socio-economic objectives.
5. Develop and implement monitoring, evaluation and learning mechanisms for open government strategies and initiatives.
6. Actively communicate about open government strategies and initiatives, as well as about their outputs, outcomes and impacts.
7. Proactively make available clear, complete, timely, reliable and relevant public sector data and information that is: free of cost; available in an open and non-proprietary machine-readable format; easy to find, understand, use and reuse; and disseminated through a multi-channel approach, to be prioritised in consultation with stakeholders.
8. Grant all stakeholders equal and fair opportunities to be informed and consulted and actively engage them in all phases of the policy cycle and service design and delivery. This should be done with adequate time and at minimal cost, while avoiding duplication to minimise consultation fatigue. Further, specific efforts should be dedicated to reaching out to the most relevant, vulnerable, under-represented, or marginalised groups in society, while avoiding undue influence and policy capture.
9. Explore innovative ways to effectively engage with stakeholders to source ideas and co-create solutions and seize the opportunities provided by digital government tools.
10. Explore the potential of moving from the concept of open government towards that of open state, while recognising the roles, prerogatives and overall independence of all concerned parties, and according to their existing legal and institutional frameworks.

Source: OECD (2017[1]), *OECD Recommendation of the Council on Open Government,* OECD/LEGAL/0438, https://legalinstruments.oecd.org/OECD-LEGAL-0438.

The OECD open government scan of Lebanon

The "OECD Open Government Scan of Lebanon" aims to support the government's efforts to build more transparent, participatory, and accountable institutions that can restore citizens' trust and promote inclusive growth. It analyses priority areas of reform in line with the 2017 *OECD Recommendation of the Council on Open Government* and provides concrete suggestions for further embedding the principles and practices of open government in policy-making cycles and evaluating their impacts. Ultimately, this analysis can serve as the foundation to define and pursue a whole-of-government vision for a more open government in Lebanon.

This *Open Government Scan of Lebanon* benefits from ongoing support and dialogue with successive Lebanese governments and the Office of the Minister of State for Administrative Reform (OMSAR), which has over the past years taken steps towards establishing a national open government agenda in Lebanon. This continuous commitment was initially affirmed by former Minister May Chidiac, who formally announced OMSAR's engagement in this process as well as the Government's intent to work towards adhering to the OECD Recommendation of the Council on Open Government and joining the Open Government Partnership, during a high-level conference co-organised with the OECD and under the patronage of the Prime Minister in June 2019.

This commitment has been re-affirmed at the beginning of 2020 by Minister Demianos Kattar, who subsequently expressed Lebanon's commitment to continue its joint work with the OECD in pursuit of an open government agenda for a more transparent, participatory, responsive, and trustworthy public administration. Building on these steps, the findings of this analysis have benefitted from the extensive review by OMSAR and from discussions with several representatives of relevant Lebanese institutions and civil society organisations as well as international organisations active in the promotion of good governance reforms Lebanon (i.e. OGP, UNDP, World Bank) and peer reviewers from Canada and Italy.

Developing a strategy or a long-term agenda is a core step towards achieving the vision of a more open government. Chapter 2 looks at how Lebanon can bring scattered open government initiatives under one roof, strengthen their coherence and gain a stronger mandate. Chapters 3 and 4 discuss framing this vision within a sound enabling environment, including a comprehensive regulatory and legal framework and as an institutional framework that supports the effective implementation of reforms and initiatives. Given that an open government agenda or strategy needs to be continually evaluated and revised, Chapter 5 discusses how Lebanese officials can ensure that they are gathering insights and evidence to measure impact.

Subsequent chapters address how Lebanese citizens are informed, engaged and brought into the decision-making process. Chapter 6 analyses how public communication is a central function of an open government and how it can increase the impact of transparency measures by providing information to the widest possible audience. As noted in Chapter 7, Lebanon has begun integrating participatory mechanisms in some of its policy processes, which can be further expanded in the future, drawing on the valuable insights of the country's strong civil society.

The final chapters of the scan provide an view of how Lebanon can integrate the concept of an "open state" into its open government vision or strategy (Chapter 8), outline the necessary steps to attain eligibility to join the OGP (Chapter 9), and institutionalise open government practices at the decentralised level, including in the municipalities of Shweir and Jbeil (Byblos) (Chapter 10).

In developing the analysis and recommendations, the open government scan has been based on an Open Government Survey to which the Government of Lebanon, under the leadership of OMSAR, replied in September 2019, and builds on a peer review mission conducted in September 2019 with the co-operation and support of then Minister of State for Administrative Reform, as well as the participation of various ministries, departments, and agencies.[2] The data collection for this report and its drafting were finalised before the explosion in the port of Beirut and the ensuing government crisis. However, Lebanese public institutions had the opportunity to review its findings during the month of August 2020 and confirmed the validity of its recommendations. The OECD is currently working with OMSAR to develop an action plan to implement them.

This scan has also benefitted from the expertise of OECD peers from Canada and Italy, namely Sarah MacLeod (Analyst/Advisor on Open Government, Office of the Chief Information Officer, Treasury Board of Canada Secretariat) and Marco Marrazza, Head of Department Office, International Relations, Presidency of Council of Ministers, Department for Public Administration. At the local level, the open government scan was developed on the basis of an OECD survey targeting Jbeil (Byblos) and Shweir, as well as interviews with mayors, councillors, municipal administration and local civil society.

Notes

1 See http://www.pcm.gov.lb/Library/Images/Hok76Ministers/w76n.pdf

2 These include representatives from the Prime Minister's Office; Ministries of Information, Finance, Interior and Municipalities, and Justice; the Court of Audit; Central Inspection Unit; the Central Administration for Statistics; the Access to Information Technical Committee; the Technology and Information Parliamentary Committee; the Higher Education Committee; the Lebanese Oil and Gas Initiative; Gherbal Initiative; the Lebanese Transparency Association; Nahnoo; and SMEX.

References

Lebanese Center for Policy Studies (2019), *Citizens Believe the Government Should Prioritize Tackling Widespread Corruption*, https://www.lcps-lebanon.org/featuredArticle.php?id=215. [5]

Lebanese Transparency Association (2019), *"How will Lebanon's "Let's get to work" government face the challenges of corruption?"*, Online article, https://voices.transparency.org/how-will-lebanons-let-s-get-to-work-government-face-the-challenges-of-corruption-4872f9bc6743. [4]

OECD (2017), *Recommendation of the Council on Open Government*, https://legalinstruments.oecd.org/en/instruments/OECD-LEGAL-0438. [1]

OECD (2016), *Open Government: The Global Context and the Way Forward*, OECD Publishing, Paris, https://dx.doi.org/10.1787/9789264268104-en. [2]

Yee, V. (2020), *"Lebanon Will Default on Foreign Debt Payment Amid Deepening Economic Crisis"*, Online article, https://www.nytimes.com/2020/03/07/world/middleeast/lebanon-debt-financial-crisis.html (accessed on 2 July 2020). [3]

Chapter 2. Towards an open government strategy

Countries worldwide have been designing and implementing open government initiatives for many decades. With the creation of the Open Government Partnership (OGP), countries have started creating open government action plans that assemble a series of initiatives, include a calendar and milestones. While action plans have enabled governments to unite several actors around the same vision and create further awareness about ongoing initiatives, they do not offer a long-term vision with strategic objectives and corresponding actions. The OECD Recommendation on Open Government (hereafter "the OECD Recommendation") therefore recommends to "take measures, in all branches and at all levels of the government, to develop and implement open government strategies and initiatives in collaboration with stakeholders and to foster commitment from politicians, members of parliament, senior public managers and public officials, to ensure successful implementation and prevent or overcome obstacles related to resistance to change" (OECD, 2017[1]).

Box 2.1. Open government strategy and initiative

An open government strategy or open government policy is "a document that defines the open government agenda of the central government and/or of any of its subnational levels, as well as that of a single public institution or thematic area, and that includes key open government initiatives, together with short, medium and long-term goals and indicators".

Open government initiatives are "actions undertaken by the government, or by a single public institution, to achieve specific objectives in the area of open government, ranging from the drafting of laws to the implementation of specific activities such as online consultations".

Source: OECD (2017[1]), *Recommendation of the Council on Open Government*, https://legalinstruments.oecd.org/en/instruments/OECD-LEGAL-0438.

In line with the principles of open government, such a strategy is ideally elaborated, implemented and evaluated as part of an inclusive process. Many countries have established open government committees (see Chapter 4) and developed a variety of participation mechanisms, such as online consultations and co-creation workshops.

Box 2.2. A participatory approach to developing Argentina's 3rd OGP Action Plan

Argentina joined the Open Government Partnership in 2012, and has enhanced its participatory approach with each new OGP Action Plan. The third plan (2017-2019) benefitted from a participatory and co-creation process including 28 government institutions, 54 civil society organisations, 11 provincial governments and 90 local civil society organisations. The process was led by a National Open Government Roundtable, created in 2017, and composed of four government institutions and four civil society organisations.

The elaboration of the action plan followed five stages: 1) idea suggestion phase through an online form and a series of meetings, coupled with an awareness-raising exercise among government institutions; 2) prioritising proposals by analysing the received ideas and categorising them according to their admissibility for the plan; 3) roundtables at national and provincial levels with government and civil society to draft commitments based on the proposals; 4) a review of the commitments by the National Open Government Roundtable; and 5) a public consultation on an online portal for comments.

Sources: OECD (2019[6]), *Open Government in Argentina*, https://dx.doi.org/10.1787/1988ccef-en; OGP (2018[7]), *OGP Participation and Co-Creation Toolkit*, www.opengovpartnership.org/stories/ogps-participation-and-co-creation-toolkit-from-usual-suspects-to-business-as-usual/.

As a first step towards creating a common vision of open government, the OECD recommends adopting a definition that unites all actors around a joint understanding of what open government aims to achieve. Such a definition can be based on the OECD Recommendation, on the definition of other international actors such as the OGP, or be the country's own creation. Some 49% of countries across the OECD have a single definition (OECD, 2016[2]). In line with this practice, Lebanon has put forth its own open government definition which states that:

> *Open government is the simple but powerful idea that governments and institutions work better for citizens when they are transparent, engaging and accountable. Open government is the major building block for a more democratic, equal and sustainable society.*

This definition was stated by the previous Minister of State for Administrative Reform, Minister Chidiac, on 24 June 2019, and has since been used as a working definition. The definition is an important step towards creating a joint vision of open government in Lebanon, and it should be widely disseminated among the public administration and citizens. This is particularly important as currently Lebanon does not have an open government strategy or action plan, but several rather independent initiatives.

Figure 2.1. Open government initiatives implemented by OECD and MENA countries

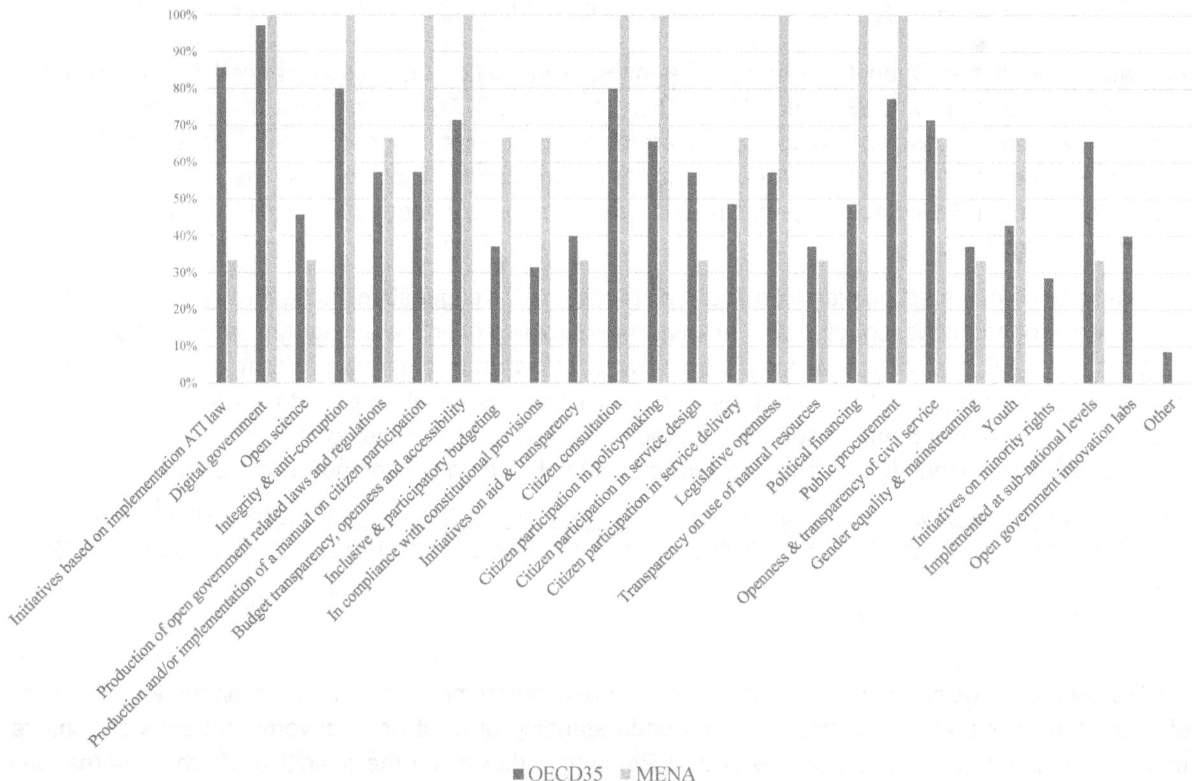

Note: MENA (Middle East and North Africa) includes Morocco, Tunisia and Jordan.
Source: OECD (2016[2]), *Open Government: The Global Context and the Way Forward*, https://doi.org/10.1787/9789264268104-en.

As in many OECD and Middle East and North Africa (MENA) countries (see Figure 2.1), before the existence of a dedicated open government strategy or action plan, open government initiatives are being implemented in Lebanon in the framework of other strategies. The most notable of these strategies are the National Anti-corruption Strategy 2020-2025 and the draft Digital Transformation Strategy 2020-2030 and related implementation plan. Both strategies and action plans make reference to open government and promote the implementation of specific open government principles.

Draft Digital Transformation Strategy

The draft 2019 Digital Transformation Strategy aims to transform the Lebanese public administration into one that harnesses digital technologies for innovation and for easier interaction with citizens. It considers a digital transformation at the heart of public service reform and provides a roadmap for how to achieve this transformation. The strategy includes open government as a focus area, highlighting that government should be based on transparency, collaboration and participation (Figure 2.2). The government strives to strengthen transparency and open data by making information accessible and clear, such as through the common portal www.lebanon.gov.lb where citizens, businesses and public sector organisations can access information on a centralised platform; by publishing government data in a high quality and open format on the open data platform www.data.gov.lb and by making processes open, which involves providing information on how processes work. The country also aims to create "digital by default" open services and be responsive to citizen feedback, which includes enhancing participation by opening up the processes and services for co-creation. In addition to the specific focus area of open government, other focus areas, such as information, common standards, digital skills and collaboration, also support the implementation of open government principles. At the time of writing, the strategy has been transformed into a draft implementation plan 2020-2030 and submitted to the Ministerial Committee for review.

Figure 2.2. Lebanon's open government approach

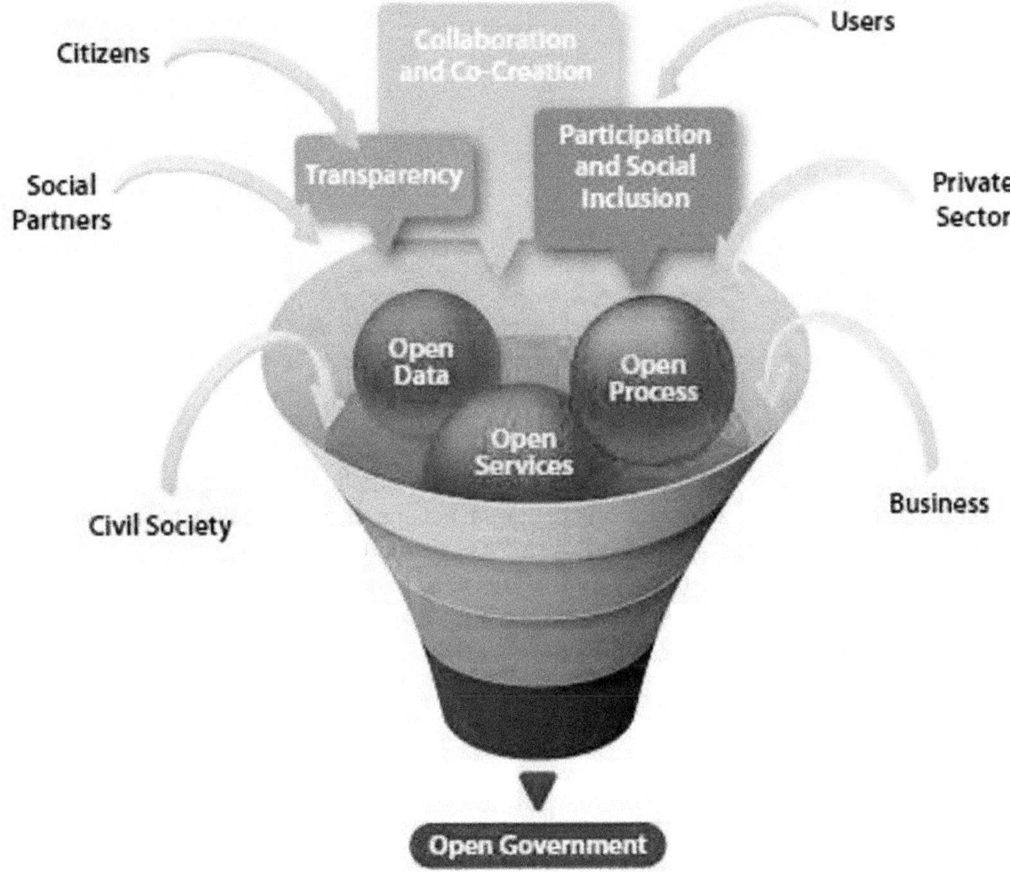

Source: Government of Lebanon (2019[8]), *Lebanon Digital Transformation: Strategies to Actions*.

The draft implementation plan also considers open government as a foundation for digital transformation, and is built on the five pillars of people, innovation, processes, civic engagement and legal framework (see Figure 2.3).

Figure 2.3. Digital transformation pillars

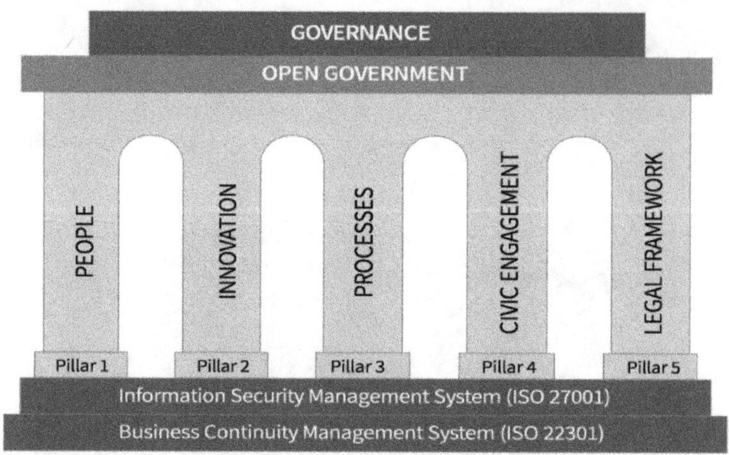

Source: Government of Lebanon (2019[8]), *Lebanon Digital Transformation: Strategies to Actions*.

Based on the digital transformation framework, the draft implementation plan includes eight programme pillars with several foreseen actions. A number of these actions contribute directly to enhancing the principles of open government as they aim to facilitate access to information, create awareness about open government among the public administration and citizens, and propose means for participation. The success in implementing the digital transformation will be measured through six key performance areas and their various sub-areas, several of which measure improvements regarding open government reform implementation (see Box 2.3). The draft implementation plan specifically mentions joining the OGP as a key performance indicator.

Box 2.3. Lebanon's draft digital transformation implementation plan 2020-2030

The draft digital transformation implementation plan's vision is "to improve the quality of life of our people and businesses by transforming Lebanon into one of the most advanced digital countries in the Arab world, ensuring a transparent open government, and implementing citizen-centric digital services so that public civil servants can better serve citizens, residents, foreign visitors, entrepreneurs and wider society" by 2030. It provides several actions that directly support the enhancement of open government principles. The most important are listed below; however, several other foreseen actions will also support open government principles more indirectly, such as the digitalisation of services.

An overview of some of the most important "open government" actions:

- Permanent consultation platform for citizens and civil society
- Implement the www.data.gov.lb Open Government and Public Administration Performance Portal
- Establish a virtual digital academy
- Open government public sector training
- The Open Government Information eXchange (OGIX) Project
- Review and reform of the legal framework, regulations and laws
- Standardise the website and mobile applications
- Document the "as is" public sector organisational structure and job descriptions and define the "to be" organisational structure
- Digital transformation public awareness campaigns
- Open government public awareness campaigns

The most important key performance sub-areas that relate to open government:

- Citizen experience with government services
- Citizen participation and engagement
- Citizen access to information
- Transparency and accountability
- Business participation and engagement
- Business access to information
- Open government data policy
- Public communications, visibility and media

Source: Government of Lebanon (2019[8]), *Lebanon Digital Transformation: Strategies to Actions.*

National Anti-corruption Strategy

Lebanon recently adopted Law No. 175/2020 on 8 May 2020 on "Fighting Corruption in the Public Sector and establishing the National Anti-corruption Institution" as well as the National Anti-Corruption Strategy 2020-2025 on 12 May 2020. As part of this strategy, the government seeks to pave the way for the future establishment and activation of the National Anti-Corruption Institution. The strategy, which was adopted by the Anti-corruption Ministerial Committee, includes “enhancing transparency,” “enabling accountability,” and “ending impunity” as its objectives. Its vision furthermore highlights the principles of integrity by calling for “a prosperous society where the rule of law and integrity prevail and a democratic, fair and transparent state that manages the affairs of the country and invests its resources in a way that meets the requirements of development, quality and modernity.”

Open government is tightly linked to implementing the access to information law, proactive disclosure of information, and the involvement of citizens in decision-making processes. As such, the mission of the National Anti-corruption Strategy recognises the importance “protecting public funds and public affairs from corruption, to safeguard the rights of citizens and provide them with a decent livelihood, through the concerted efforts of the legislative, executive and judicial authorities and with the participation of public administrations, institutions, municipalities, trade unions, civil society, the private sector and the media.” (Republic of Lebanon, n.d.[9]) The implementation framework includes seven outcomes with several outputs and areas of work that directly contribute to open government initiatives (see Box 2.4).

Box 2.4. The National Anti-corruption Strategy Implementation Framework

The implementation framework of the National Anti-corruption Strategy includes a set of outputs that support open government initiatives, the most important are:

1. Completing and activating specialised anti-corruption legislation (including the Right of Access to Information law):
    - Creation and operationalisation of the national anti-corruption authority.
    - Establishment of an effective system for financial disclosure and anti-illicit enrichment.
    - Encouragement and protection of anti-corruption whistleblowers.
    - Establishment of an effective system for managing conflict of interests.
    - Promotion of compliance with the law on the Right of Access to Information.
2. Protecting the integrity of human resources management for the public sector.
    - Establishment of a comprehensive system to promote ethical conduct in public administration
3. Enhancing the integrity of the public procurement system.
4. Supporting the role of the judicial system in combating corruption:
    - Strengthened transparency in court administration and related departments.
5. Supporting the role of oversight and inspection bodies in combating corruption:
    - Supporting the implementation of the law on the Ombudsman of the Republic.
6. Promoting community participation in disseminating a culture of integrity:
    - Raising of citizen awareness on the impact of corruption and their role in rejecting it.
    - Investment in future generations through education and teaching.
    - Non-governmental organisations empowered to play a constructive role in promoting a culture of integrity.
    - Enhancement of the capacity of journalists to work on revealing instances of corruption and providing coverage of related reform efforts.
7. Integrating preventive measures against corruption at the sectoral level:
    - Enhancement of transparency in the interface between public administration and users of public services.
    - Implementation of selected measures to enhance transparency and accountability in prioritised sectors.

Developing an open government action plan

While the Digital Transformation Strategy and the National Anti-corruption Strategy, and their respective action plans, are the most important strategic documents linked to open government, several other ongoing public sector reforms include open government initiatives. Notably, these include the national action plan for the implementation of the Right of Access to Information law (discussed in Chapter 3), the ongoing reforms regarding human resources (see Chapter 4), efforts to strengthen public sector procurement transparency and accountability, as well as OMSAR's co-operation with the Central Inspection Board regarding the development of key performance indicators for the public sector, some of which aim to measure the implementation of open government principles.

Thus, even though there is no national open government strategy, Lebanon is already implementing a variety of open government initiatives, and has included several more in its strategic documents. In order to build awareness among the public administration and create a common vision of open government, as well as to inform citizens about ongoing initiatives, Lebanon could consider elaborating an open government action plan. This plan would build upon the abovementioned definition of open government and regroup all ongoing and planned open government related initiatives. The plan could be made public and be widely disseminated to all public administrations. It could be used to report regularly on implementation progress to all concerned stakeholders. While this approach does not call for the elaboration of more ambitious reforms, it could be a first step to building an open government community and awareness within and outside the public administration. This action plan could be updated through an inclusive process after a certain period (for example one year) to include new and more ambitious actions. It could be managed by OMSAR's open government team, receive strategic direction from the sub-committee on open government, and could be elaborated through a process involving the recommended open government forum (see Chapter 4).

Box 2.5. The Open Government Strategy of the Province of Alberta (Canada)

The Open Government Strategy of the Province of Alberta in Canada is structured as follows:

- **Vision**: the main objective of the strategy.
- **Mission statement**: an explanation of the identified vision and the province's definition of open government.
- **Drivers**: five key elements that motivated the province to design the strategy, including "A wealth of new digital opportunities transforming everyday life for many citizens and companies."
- **Goals**: four key objectives and related sub-objectives, including "the public service working together with citizens to make government more responsive to meeting the evolving needs of Albertans".
- **Outcomes**: five main intended results, including "increased transparency" and related measures of success such as "increased freedom of information requests".
- **Principles**: three principles that guide the implementation of the strategy, including "open by design".
- **Activity streams**: three "streams" of effort identified by the government, including concrete commitments and ministry accountabilities.

Source: Province of Alberta (n.d.[10]), *Open Government Strategy*, https://open.alberta.ca/documentation/strategic-plan.

Recommendation:

- **Elaborate an open government action plan that would group all ongoing and planned open government related initiatives into a common approach in order to foster an open government culture and stakeholder community inside and outside the public administration.**
- **Disseminate the open government action plan and the open government definition to the public and the public administration as well as inform them regularly about implementation progress.**

Going forward, update the open government action plan with more ambitious commitments developed through an inclusive process and eventually transform it into an open government strategy.

References

Government of Lebanon (2019), *Lebanon Digital Transformation: Strategies to Actions.* [5]

OECD (2019), *Open Government in Argentina*, OECD Public Governance Reviews, OECD Publishing, Paris, https://dx.doi.org/10.1787/1988ccef-en. [2]

OECD (2017), *Recommendation of the Council on Open Government*, https://legalinstruments.oecd.org/en/instruments/OECD-LEGAL-0438. [1]

OECD (2016), *Open Government: The Global Context and the Way Forward*, OECD Publishing, Paris, https://dx.doi.org/10.1787/9789264268104-en. [4]

OGP (2018), *OGP Participation and Co-Creation Toolkit*, Open Government Partnership, https://www.opengovpartnership.org/stories/ogps-participation-and-co-creation-toolkit-from-usual-suspects-to-business-as-usual/ (accessed on 15 November 2019). [3]

Province of Alberta (n.d.), *Open Government Strategy*, https://open.alberta.ca/documentation/strategic-plan. [7]

Republic of Lebanon (n.d.), *National Anti-corruption Strategy 2020-2025.* [6]

Chapter 3. Legal framework

A robust legal framework that guarantees rights regarding accessing information and civic space, and enables possibilities for participation and accountability, is a pre-condition for designing and implementing open government initiatives. These legal and regulatory prerequisites determine the rules, rights and obligations of all stakeholders involved and provides a common framework. Ideally it is elaborated through an inclusive process and is transparent, widely communicated and accessible. The OECD Recommendation on Open Government recommends "ensuring the existence and implementation of the necessary open government legal and regulatory framework, including through the provision of supporting documents such as guidelines and manuals, while establishing adequate oversight mechanisms to ensure compliance" (Provision 2).

Lebanon's legal framework builds on its Constitution, which states that "Lebanon is a parliamentary democratic republic based on respect for public liberties, especially the freedom of opinion and belief, and respect for social justice and equality of rights and duties among all citizens without discrimination" (preamble). More specifically, Article 13 guarantees core civil liberties, such as the freedoms of expression, of press, of association and of assembly.

In recent years, the country has adopted several pieces of legislation to further define the legal framework that is relevant to open government. These include the Right of Access to Information Law (No. 28 dated 10 February 2017), the Illicit Enrichment Law (No. 154 dated 27 December 1999), the Whistleblower Protection Law (No. 83 of 10 October 2018), the Electronic Transactions and Personal Data Protection Law No. 81/2018, and Law No. 84/2018 on Strengthening Transparency in the Oil and Gas Sector. Most recently, Lebanon adopted Law No. 175/2020 on Fighting Corruption in the Public Sector and the National Anti-corruption Strategy 2020-2025, which paves the way for the future establishment of the National Anti-corruption Institution, as well as the Law on Asset and Interest Declaration and the Fight against Illicit Enrichment, which was adopted on 30 September 2020.

Access to information

The adoption of the Right of Access to Information Law in 2017 following a long process, which started in 2004 and was spearheaded by a National Network for the Right of Access to Information, was an important milestone towards greater transparency and open government. Such laws are considered a key pillar of democratic governance and open government, and are common practice in OECD countries, with all but one having such a law. Access to information enables stakeholders to scrutinise government, hold it accountable and participate in policy-making processes in a more informed manner. Moreover, it can increase citizens' trust in government and is a tool to prevent and fight corruption (OECD, 2019[6]). Accessing information mainly occurs through two means: the proactive disclosure and publication of information by public institutions, and the provision of information upon an access to information request. Lebanon's law provides for both means of accessing information. Article 1 states that "every person, natural or legal" has the right to access information, while Article 7 details the documents that have to be published proactively, which include "decisions, instructions, circulars, and memoranda that include an interpretation of laws and regulations or that are of a regulatory nature" as well as "all transactions involving payment of more than LBP 5 000 000 [Lebanese pound] of public funds". In addition, all public institutions are obliged to produce and publish an annual report about their activities. The Lebanese law enshrines further obligations on the administration, namely explaining non-regulatory administrative decisions (Article 11) and publishing the rationale behind laws. The law allows for the use and reuse of the information, except for commercial purposes. It covers a wide range of public institutions, thereby creating a solid basis for accessing information. At the same time it includes exceptions without putting them under a "harm" or "public interest" test, as is common practice in OECD countries. Implementation practice and the current draft implementation decree should ensure that these exceptions do not hinder effective access to information.

While the Right of Access to Information law could be further aligned with international standards, the implementation of the current law is the most important step to further a transparency culture in Lebanon and enhance the implementation of open government principles. Recent studies from civil society organisations show that despite the access to implementation law having been in place for over two years, more effort is needed regarding implementation. A study conducted by the Gherbal Initiative in 2018 showed that only 26% of the institutions they made an access to information request to answered this request. The Gherbal Initiative then undertook another study in 2019 in which they requested the 2017 financial statements of 140 institutions, this also showed that the public administration is not yet fully complying with the law: 120 institutions received the request, of which 52 refused to provide the information, 29 gave incomplete answers, 6 said they do not have a budget and only 33 provided the full information (Gherbal Initiative, 2019[11]).

As a result, OECD supported OMSAR in developing a National Action Plan on the Implementation of the Right of Access to Information law and is currently supporting its implementation. The plan was elaborated by a Technical Access to Information Committee and was adopted by the Anti-corruption Ministerial Committee. It has benefitted from a wide range of consultations with civil society members, media, local government, public officials, parliamentarians, the justice sector and the private sector. The 10 implementation areas provide for a comprehensive approach to implementation of the law, could greatly advance transparency in Lebanon (see Box 3.1). OMSAR is currently elaborating key performance indicators to monitor implementation of the plan. These monitoring results should be made publicly available, while the involvement of various stakeholders in the monitoring process would also further strengthen the adoption of open government principles. Going forward, OMSAR is working to develop an access to information e-portal to assist obligated administrations in the proactive disclosure of information to the public.

In addition to these efforts, Expertise France is working with the Ministry of Environment to implement pilot projects on accessing information, according to the OECD survey. In September 2019, OMSAR, together with the OECD and UNDP, organised a workshop on the role of information officers in enforcing the Right of Access to Information law. Approximately 100 public officials attended the workshop, and the ministry is currently following up with government entities to check whether these public officials have been appointed as information officers in an effort to create a network of such officers.

Box 3.1. National action plan for implementing the Right of Access to Information Law

OECD supported OMSAR in developing a National Action Plan on the Implementation of the Right of Access to Information law and is currently supporting its implementation.

A national stakeholder workshop was jointly organised with OMSAR and UNDP in June 2019 to discuss the draft national action plan. The workshop brought together representatives of the public administration, parliamentarians, civil society organisations, media and the private sector to consult on the draft national action plan and discuss its different activities. The plan will be adopted by the Ministerial Anti-corruption Committee.

Summary of the activities foreseen by the action plan:

1. Develop a comprehensive list of the obligated administrations by the ATI Law.
2. Appoint ATI officers (ATIO) within all obligated administrations.
3. Provide information about ATI rights and procedures.
4. Provide training and support.
5. Develop electronic tools to implement the ATI law.
6. Appoint the National Anti-corruption Institution (NACI).
7. Develop oversight mechanisms to ensure the compliance of the obligated administrations.
8. Implement mechanisms for receiving and handling complaints related to ATI implementation.
9. Issue implementation decrees in areas of necessity.
10. Develop open and effective filing and archiving systems.

As is the case in several OECD countries, the Right of Access to Information law foresees the establishment of a body to oversee the implementation of the law, provide education about the law, and receive and treat complaints regarding its implementation. In Lebanon, this body will be the National Anti-corruption Institution, which is expected to be an independent body that will ensure the adequate implementation of the law. Until this institution is formally established, complaints can only be addressed to the courts, namely the Council of State, which often involves long and costly procedures.

Lebanon has passed another law regarding accessing information in a specific sector: Law No. 84/2018 Strengthening Transparency in the Oil and Gas Sector.[1] This law aims to combat corruption by establishing transparency mechanisms in the petroleum sector. Article 4 of the law calls for the proactive disclosure of information regarding all petroleum activities on a quarterly basis. Article 19 assigns the Anti-corruption Institution with the responsibility of ensuring the effective implementation of the law. According to this provision, the Institution has the duty to monitor the appropriateness, credibility and quality of information relevant to the petroleum industry. In addition, this article calls on the Institution to publish annual reports highlighting the significant difficulties witnessed by people in accessing information on the petroleum industry, which would be submitted to the Council of Ministers and Parliament.

Anti-corruption and integrity legislation

Integrity is one of the key principles of open government, and therefore the adoption of a range of legislation in the field of anti-corruption and integrity is common practice to support an open government culture and a solid open government legal framework. Lebanon recently adopted Law No. 175/2020 on 8 May 2020 on "Fighting Corruption in the Public Sector and establishing the National Anti-corruption Institution" as well as the National Anti-Corruption Strategy 2020-2025 on 12 May 2020 that includes 34 outputs. As part of this strategy, the government seeks to pave the way for the future establishment and activation of the National Anti-Corruption Institution.

In addition to this landmark anti-corruption legislation, Lebanon has committed to make efforts in this field, and ratified the United Nations Convention against Corruption (UNCAC) on 22 April 2009. Likewise, the 2009 Illicit Enrichment Law specifies the categories of public officials that should disclose their assets when they take office (Article 2), identifies the parties entrusted with receiving financial declarations according to the rank of the public official, as disclosures are not made public in the country (Article 5), and outlines the procedures for prosecution in cases of illicit enrichment (Article 10). However, this law does not list illicit enrichment as a crime by itself. Accordingly, an updated Law on Asset and Interest Declaration and the Fight against Illicit Enrichment was adopted on 30 September 2020, which further specifics the scope and obligations related to asset disclosures of public officials.

In addition to these laws and in line with UNCAC, Lebanon passed a law to protect whistleblowers (Law No. 83 of 2018 on protecting whistleblowers) as well as a number of additional laws, directives and decisions that support the anti-corruption legal framework. These include, among others: the Law on Lifting bank secrecy; Law No. 44 of 24/11/2015 on Fighting Money Laundering and Terrorist Financing; Law of Appointments of First and Second-category Positions; Law No. 42 of 24/11/2015 on the Declaration on Transfer of Funds Across Borders; Ombudsman Law No. 664 of 4/2/2005; Law No. 25 of 27/10/ 2016 on Exchange of Tax Information; Law No. 48 of 9/7/2017 on Public Private Partnership; and Penal code No. 340 of 1/3/1943 and its amendments. Finally, a code of ethics for public procurement officials provides some integrity principles to be respected. Wide dissemination of the code would further enshrine the respect of these principles within the public administration.

Digital government legislation

In line with Provision 9 of the OECD Recommendation, digital government tools provide opportunities to source ideas and co-create solutions. To enable digital tools to play this role, the appropriate legislative frameworks are needed. The Electronic Transactions and Personal Data Protection Law No. 81/2018 presents a first step in this direction as it sets the foundation for e-services and e-engagement portals, and states that "information technology is at the service of the people" (Article 2). The Government of Lebanon should continue the efforts underway to keep its legal and regulatory frameworks updated in critical areas such as the digital rights of citizens and businesses. At the same time, enhancing the digital transformation of the public sector is not a static process, as the fast pace of digital technological development requires governments to be able to permanently adapt to new contexts, drivers and expectations from citizens and businesses. Lebanon should in this sense prioritise the development of an agile, collaborative and experimental culture across the administration that can go beyond legalistic approaches.

Stakeholder engagement legislation

Circular No. 21/2012 of 25 August 2012 requires all public entities to publish draft legal texts on government websites and solicit consultation and feedback from stakeholders, including civil society. Public entities are required by this circular to assess the feedback received from consultations and integrate this feedback as necessary into updated versions of the legal texts. This includes draft laws, draft decrees, draft policies and sectoral strategies. The circular also specifies that public entities should publish draft legal texts for 15 days and immediately notify stakeholders (academia, civil society, media, etc.). This is a necessary prerequisite to presenting these texts to the Council of Ministers, and a civil servant should be appointed in each public entity to manage this process.

OECD countries are moving towards greater stakeholder engagement, and are at least developing guidelines to support public institutions in this process. The purpose of these guidelines is to create a common framework for public officials and stakeholders that defines common rules, rights and obligations.

Examples include the United Kingdom's guide "Ensuring Effective Stakeholder Engagement", or the citizen participation charter developed by the municipality of Paris through a co-creation and inclusive process (see Box 3.2).

Box 3.2. Stakeholder engagement guidelines

United Kingdom

"Ensuring Effective Stakeholder Engagement" is a guide to help run, manage and evaluate stakeholder campaigns developed by the Department for Business, Innovation and Skills of the United Kingdom. It includes the following sections:

- Introduction that explains stakeholder engagement
- Getting started
- Identification: Which stakeholders are critical to your success?
- Putting together an engagement plan: How are you going to engage with them?
- Implementation: Evaluation — did you achieve your objectives?

Canada

The Government of Canada has rules of engagement for online engagement, which highlight how the government reacts to comments and interacts with citizens, when they should remove comments, and the terms of replying. In addition, public engagement principles highlight the principles that the government is committed to respect when engaging with citizens. These include: transparency, relevance, inclusiveness, accountability and adaptability.

City of Paris

The Paris Charter for Citizen Participation was adopted in 2017 following an inclusive development process. It is based on a previous charter that was improved to take into account the experiences of the first version. It includes the following sections:

- What participation means
- Open and inclusive participation
- Participation known by all
- More understandable participation
- Transparency and a participation contract
- Renewing citizens' institutions
- Strengthening the citizens' role in municipality affairs
- Fostering agoras and public sector innovation
- Create a long-term participatory culture
- Promote the charter

Source: Department for Business, Innovation and Skills (n.d.[12]), *Ensuring Effective Stakeholder Engagement*, https://gcs.civilservice.gov.uk/publications/ensuring-effective-stakeholder-engagement/; Mairie de Paris (2017[13]), Paris Citizen Participation Charter, https://cdn.paris.fr/paris/2019/07/24/7e858177d8e8e9f59e6804e3b82994eb.pdf; Government of Canada (2020[14]), Rules of Engagement, https://open.canada.ca/en/rules-engagement; Government of Canada (n.d.[15]), Principles and Guidelines, https://open.canada.ca/en/content/principles-and-guidelines.

Lebanon has initiated some steps in this direction with its work on regulatory impact assessments (RIA) and a circular on consultation. In particular, OMSAR developed guidelines for conducting RIA, which include guidelines for engaging citizens in this process, in particular through consultation. The guidelines highlight the different steps to undertake, which include: planning early consultations, identification of stakeholders, and preparation of necessary documents and implementation of consultation methods specific to each stakeholder. The Economic and Social Council (ECOSOC), which works as an advisory body to the Council of Ministers, is expected to play an important role in the RIA process as it acts as a main platform for dialogue between public and private actors.

Some countries are going a step further and enshrining participatory rights in their legislative framework. Article 14 of Argentina's Constitution, for example, recognises the "right to petition the authorities" (OECD, 2019[6]), while Tunisia's Code for Local Authorities includes a whole chapter dedicated to open government and participatory democracy at the local level (OECD, 2019[16]). Building upon this work and best practices from OECD countries, Lebanon could consider elaborating guidelines on stakeholder participation beyond regulatory consultation, and could provide a common framework to all public officials and stakeholders interested in participating. The framework could be disseminated widely and be coupled with offline and online training courses, for example using OMSAR's existing e-learning portal.

Civic space

In order to promote stakeholder participation, the space in which these interactions take place and in which citizens participate and express themselves needs to be protected and promoted. Lebanon has a vibrant civil society with more than 8 000 organisations registered as of 2014, in addition to youth and sports clubs (Division for Sustainable Development Goals, 2018[17]). Civil society organisations (CSOs) have been very vocal and engaged in promoting policy reforms, as was visible during the "You Stink" Movement in 2015 in response to the garbage crisis. There are also well-established organisations in the field of public governance, such as the Lebanese Chapter of Transparency International. CSOs and citizens have the right to protest and assemble. However, while the Constitution guarantees freedom of association, and the 1909 Law on Associations is considered enabling, organisations still face some challenges, such as delays in receiving their documents for registration. A 2006 ministerial circular requires that a receipt must be given within 30 days; however, CSOs continue to face delays (ICNL, 2019[18]). Civicus judges Lebanon's civic space as "obstructed", which refers to it being "heavily contested by power holders, who impose a combination of legal and practical constraints on the full enjoyment of fundamental rights" (Civicus, 2019[19]). Similarly, V-Democracy Values give Lebanon 2.72/4 in the category CSO entry and exit, 2.6/4 in participatory environment, and 2.5/4 in CSO repression (V-Dem Institute, 2018[20]). Although Lebanon passes the OGP's values-check, improvements in the civic space environment would encourage further dialogue between government and civil society and enhance effective stakeholder participation. The programme Afkar[3] is relevant in this context. Financed by the European Union and managed by OMSAR, the programme aimed to further strengthen civil society in Lebanon. Afkar II had a budget of EUR 3 million and focused on rule of law and national dialogue. Civil society could apply to grants for projects in the main focus areas. According to public officials, Afkar III (EUR 10 million budget) included as outputs the establishment of a policy dialogue platform and detailed guidance, with several pilots already implemented.

Freedom of the press is equally guaranteed by the Constitution, and Lebanon has a diverse media sector, despite it being politicised (RSF, 2020[21]). However, the penal code and the audio-visual media law criminalise defamation against public officials, the president and the Lebanese flag, and have been used against journalists and activists (AbiYaghi, Yammine and Jagarnathsingh, 2019[22]).

Recommendations:

- **Continue efforts underway to establish and update effective legal and regulatory frameworks for the digital transformation of the public sector**. In doing so, provide support for an agile, collaborative and experimental culture across the administration that can go beyond legalistic approaches.
- **Building on previous experience, OMSAR could elaborate stakeholder engagement guidelines that provide step-by-step guidance and an overview of different engagement tools.** In doing so, the government could disseminate these guidelines widely to the public administration and provide training courses on their application, for example, through the existing e-learning portal.

Notes

[1] https://www.lp.gov.lb/Resources/Files/e4e48ec4-1820-4200-b8b4-b9b00a3012da.pdf

[2] http://afkar.omsar.gov.lb.

References

AbiYaghi, M., L. Yammine and A. Jagarnathsingh (2019), "Civil Society in Lebanon: the Implementation Trap", *Civil Society Knowledge Centre*, Vol. 1/1, http://dx.doi.org/10.28943/cskc.002.70000. [13]

Civicus (2019), *Lebanon: Live Rating*, https://monitor.civicus.org/country/lebanon/ (accessed on 29 October 2019). [10]

Department for Business, Innovation and Skills (n.d.), *Ensuring Effective Stakeholder Engagement*, https://gcs.civilservice.gov.uk/publications/ensuring-effective-stakeholder-engagement/ (accessed on 29 October 2019). [3]

Division for Sustainable Development Goals (2018), *Lebanon: Voluntary National Review on Sustainable Development Goals*, United Nations, https://sustainabledevelopment.un.org/content/documents/19484Lebanon_VNR_2018.pdf (accessed on 29 October 2019). [8]

Gherbal Initiative (2019), *Transparency in Lebanese Public Administrations*, http://elgherbal.org/projects/view/en/8 (accessed on 29 October 2019). [2]

Government of Canada (2020), *"Rules of Engagement" webpage*, https://open.canada.ca/en/rules-engagement (accessed on 2 July 2020). [5]

Government of Canada (n.d.), *Principles and Guidelines*, https://open.canada.ca/en/content/principles-and-guidelines (accessed on 20 November 2019). [6]

ICNL (2019), *Lebanon - Civic Freedom Monitor*, http://www.icnl.org/research/monitor/lebanon.html (accessed on 29 October 2019). [9]

Mairie de Paris (2017), *Paris Citizen Participation Charter*, https://cdn.paris.fr/paris/2019/07/24/7e858177d8e8e9f59e6804e3b82994eb.pdf (accessed on 29 October 2019). [4]

OECD (2019), *Open Government in Argentina*, OECD Public Governance Reviews, OECD Publishing, Paris, https://dx.doi.org/10.1787/1988ccef-en. [1]

OECD (2019), *Open Government in Tunisia: La Marsa, Sayada and Sfax*, OECD Public Governance Reviews, OECD Publishing, Paris, https://dx.doi.org/10.1787/9789264310995-en. [7]

RSF (2020), *"Liban" webpage*, https://rsf.org/fr/liban (accessed on 2 July 2020). [12]

V-Dem Institute (2018), *Varieties of Democracy*, https://www.v-dem.net/en/analysis/MapGraph/ (accessed on 29 October 2019). [11]

Chapter 4. Institutional framework

Open government is a culture of governance that aims to transform how the public administration works and interacts with its citizens. The transversal nature of open government strategies and initiatives requires an effective governance structure with appropriate co-ordination mechanisms at horizontal and vertical levels. Therefore, the OECD Recommendations advise countries to "co-ordinate, through the necessary institutional mechanisms, open government strategies and initiatives – horizontally and vertically – across all levels of government to ensure that they are aligned with and contribute to all relevant socio-economic objectives" (Provision 3). Ideally, such a governance structure includes the following two aspects:

- An **Open Government Committee** that co-ordinates the national open government agenda and involves all relevant stakeholders from government, civil society, academia and the private sector.
- A **central government institution** that has a clear mandate and the capacity to steer and lead the national open government agenda (OECD, 2019[6]).

Data from OECD countries show that establishing a co-ordination unit within a central government institution is a common practice, with 77% of OECD countries having a dedicated office responsible for the horizontal co-ordination of open government initiatives. In the majority of cases (62%), this office is located in the office of the head of government or in the cabinet office/chancellery/council of ministers. This ensures high-level support and steering of open government initiatives. Ministries of finance, interior or public administration are also other common offices that take on the open government co-ordination function. The responsibilities of such an office vary (see Figure 4.1), but generally include the co-ordination function, the responsibility to develop an open government strategy, monitoring implementation, communicating reforms and in some cases assigning financial resources and evaluation of impact.

Figure 4.1. Responsibilities of the co-ordinating office

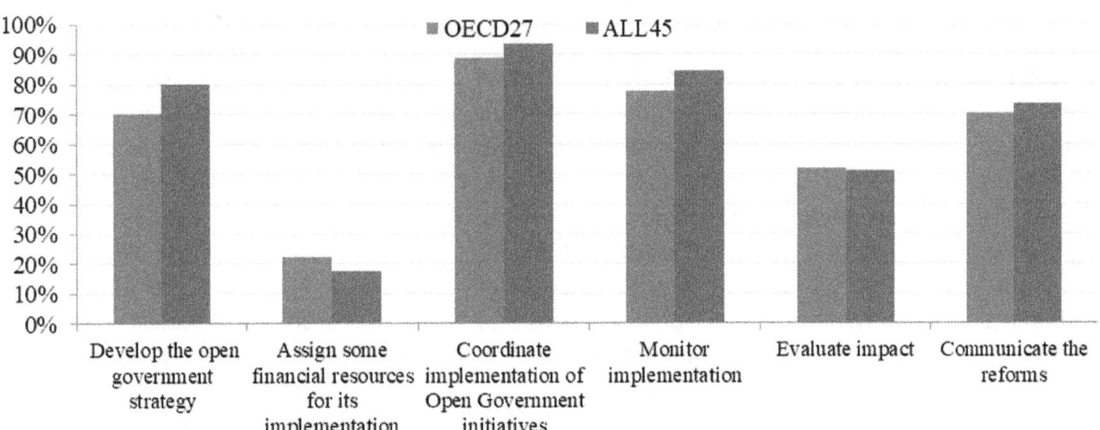

Source: OECD (2016[2])s, *Open Government: The Global Context and the Way Forward,* https://doi.org/10.1787/9789264268104-en.

Some 34% of OECD countries have also established an open government steering committee (which is equally a recommendation of the OGP), to ensure regular engagement with a variety of stakeholders. This engagement can take the form of regular communication, consultation and sometimes even co-creation, co-implementation and co-evaluation of open government initiatives. In most cases, an open government steering committee includes civil society organisations working in related fields, but local government representatives, media, private sector, trade unions or other branches of power can also be members of such a committee (OECD, 2016[2]).

Box 4.1. Composition of mixed open government forums

The establishment of a multi-stakeholder forum, following the practice in several countries, has become a mandatory feature for OGP participating countries. The OGP defines it as "a mandatory, standing consultative body that assists in this process, and is a cornerstone of each participating government's successful participation in the OGP process. It should meet every three months in order to comply with basic guidance."

A common feature of these forums is equal representation between government institutions and civil society, with civil society representatives either chosen through an open competitive process (i.e. Morocco) or a self-selection process led by civil society and often including predefined criteria (i.e. Tunisia and Canada).

These forums have several tasks while they accompany the OGP process or open government programme of a specific government. In Tunisia, the committee leads the consultation process of the OGP action plan and co-implements some commitments. In Paraguay, the forum promotes its work and the open government agenda, and also opens its meetings to the public (among others via live streaming). In Canada, the forum is governed by Terms of Reference that outline the mission, meeting frequency (every two months and extraordinary meetings) and processes to follow to avoid conflict of interest, which ensures the integrity of the forum. The forum is involved in all steps of the OGP process (action plan drafting, implementation, self-assessment and Independent Reporting Mechanism).

Source: OECD (2016[23]), *Open Government in Tunisia*, https://dx.doi.org/10.1787/9789264227118-en; OGP (2019[24]), *OGP Handbook Rules and Guidance for Participants*, www.opengovpartnership.org/wp-content/uploads/2019/03/OGP_Handbook-Rules-Guidance-for-Participants_20190313.pdf; OGP (2018[7]), *OGP Participation and Co-Creation Toolkit*, www.opengovpartnership.org/stories/ogps-participation-and-co-creation-toolkit-from-usual-suspects-to-business-as-usual/; Government of Canada (n.d.[25]), *Multi-stakeholder Forum Terms of Reference*, https://docs.google.com/document/d/1NHSHqGDQBEuY76d5VA3lcz-AtaMegyUa6C7XE9DKQv0/edit.

Lebanon's open government governance structure is still in development. OMSAR, as the ministry responsible for developing administrative reform and the institutional capacities of the public administration has taken the lead role in promoting and co-ordinating open government initiatives. For example, the minister has publicly announced Lebanon's intention to join the OGP, and OMSAR has elaborated Lebanon's definition of open government and is co-ordinating work with international institutions in this field. The OECD survey found that to support this work OMSAR has established a technical internal open government team with six public officials that unite a variety of policy areas, such as digital government and ICT, anti-corruption, human resources, legal advisors and public procurement specialists. This is a laudable step and could be reinforced by defining the responsibilities and tasks of the team.

Box 4.2. Co-ordination of open government reforms in Canada

In Canada, the Open Government Co-ordination Unit is attached to the Office of the Chief Information Officer, which is part of the Treasury Board of Canada Secretariat (TBS). In this role, it advises the Treasury Board Committee of Ministers, which manages the government's expenses on programmes and services. The work of the unit covers all stages of the policy cycle. Each of its divisions has clear responsibilities for different aspects of an effective horizontal and vertical co-ordination of open government initiatives.

The Strategic Policy and Planning Division plans, implements and reports on Canada's open government initiatives. In this respect, it aligns ongoing initiatives to increase coherence across government and complements them with additional measures in response to newly emerging challenges. The main output is Canada's National OGP Action Plan (NAP), which includes specific commitments by the Canadian government. Furthermore, the division monitors the progress of implementation of the NAP and assesses the current state of open government in Canada. The information it collects is then shared via an online tool, the quarterly updated "Progress Tracker".

The Program Implementation and International Relations Division has two areas of focus: first, it aims to increase effectiveness by improving collaboration in the framework of the Open Government Partnership with the OECD and other international partners. For example, it is the main support for the official open government point of contact. Second, it supports domestic structures in their work by providing secretariat functions and strategic guidance. For example, it leads the co-ordination of reporting on NAP commitments.

The Outreach and Engagement Division is the focal point of communication between the Government of Canada's open government work and external stakeholders and other governmental agencies and civil servants. To develop an encompassing education for civil servants, co-operation with the Canada School of Public Service has led to projects such as the Digital Academy and the corresponding "Busrides" podcasts, which provide concise supplementary information. In terms of communication with external stakeholders, one work stream covers the creation of informative content for social media, websites, presentations etc. to increase the visibility of open government. One important aspect is engagement in developing and disseminating a suitable narrative behind open government in order to motivate stakeholder participation. In this respect, the Outreach and Engagement Division aims to serve as an example for other government agencies in how it manages consultation with civil society as part of the 2020-2022 National Action Plan.

Source: Treasury Board of Canada Secretariat (n.d.[26]), *Open Government Team: Work packages*, unpublished draft; Government of Canada (2020[27]), "Open Government" webpage, **https://open.canada.ca/en**; Canada School of Public Service Digital Academy (2020[28]), "Busrides" webpage, **https://busrides-trajetsenbus.ca/en/ep-3-en/**; Kathryn May (2018[29]), "Feds launch 'digital academy' for public service", iPolitics online, **https://ipolitics.ca/2018/10/18/feds-launch-new-digital-academy-for-ps-to-help-drive-technology-makeover/.**

There is currently no mechanism to co-ordinate open government horizontally and vertically in Lebanon. However, the country, and in particular OMSAR, could build on several existing co-ordination frameworks in related policy fields that could be an inspiration or provide a structure for an open government co-ordination mechanism.

The Prime Minister's Decision No. 156/2011 established an Anti-corruption Ministerial Committee of which the Minister of State for Administrative Reform is the vice president and the Prime Minister the president. It also includes the Minister of Justice, Minister of Interior and Municipalities, and the Minister of Finance. The committee is supported by a Technical Committee (established by Prime Minister's Decision No.

156/2011) presided over by OMSAR. It is responsible for the elaboration and adoption of Lebanon's policies in the field of anti-corruption and integrity, in particular the adoption of the national anti-corruption strategy (see Chapter 2). In order to enhance the implementation of the Right of Access to Information law, and given that access to information is also a key pillar for anti-corruption, the Prime Minister formed a committee to develop the national action plan for the implementation of the Right of Access to Information law (see Chapter 3). The committee, which is composed of the Ministry of Justice, Council of State, Central Inspection Board and OMSAR, acts as a sub-committee of the Anti-corruption Ministerial Committee, which adopts its policies and action plans. Lebanon could consider establishing a sub-committee on open government that reports to the Anti-corruption Ministerial Committee and includes the members of, or co-ordinates closely with, the Access to Information Committee.

In parallel, the Lebanese Council of Ministers has established a Ministerial Committee for Digital Economy and Digital Transformation, chaired by the Prime Minister and formed by Decision No. 53 of February 28, 2019 and Decision No. 4 of May 24, 2019. As Figure 4.2 shows, the committee has various sub-structures for the implementation of policies, and is also aiming to set-up an advisory board to engage with different public and private actors.

Figure 4.2. Digital transformation structure in Lebanon

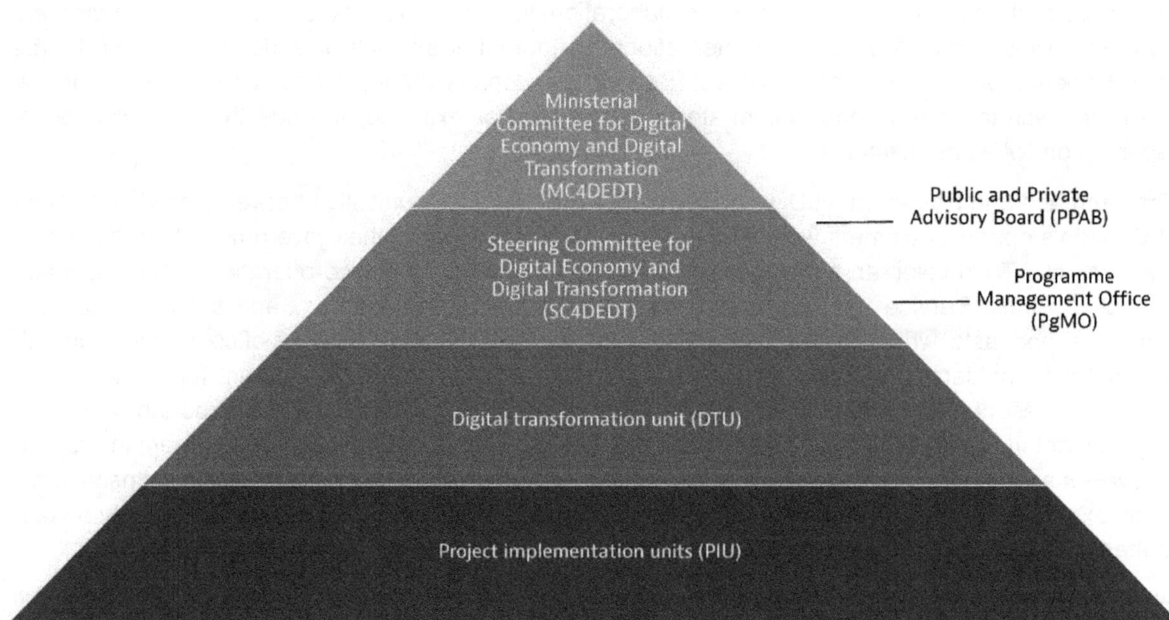

Source: Government of Lebanon (2019[8]), *Lebanon Digital Transformation: Strategies to Actions*.

According to the OECD Recommendation on Open Government, digital tools are a lever and opportunity to design and implement open government strategies and initiatives (OECD, 2017[1]). Equally, the OECD Recommendation on Digital Government Strategies promotes "capturing the value of digital technologies for more open, participatory and innovative governments" (OECD, 2019[30]). In line with these recommendations, Lebanon's digital transformation strategy lists open government as a founding principle. Hence, close co-ordination through a co-ordination mechanism on open government and the Ministerial Committee for Digital Economy and Digital Transformation, as well as its sub-bodies, is recommended. Lebanon could, for example, consider including a high-level representative of the entity responsible for leading and co-ordinating the digital government policy (e.g. OMSAR or eventually the future Lebanese

Digital Agency) in the open government committee, while having its decisions presented to or even approved by the ministerial committee.

In parallel, two other initiatives are underway to engage stakeholders in policy making. These include the Public and Private Advisory Board (mentioned in Figure 4.2) to be created in relation to the digital transformation, and a multi-stakeholder group to be created in the framework of Lebanon's intention to join the Extractive Industries Transparency Initiative (EITI). The latter is an EITI requirement and must include representatives from government, extractive companies and civil society. It will support Lebanon in meeting the standards and oversee the implementation of EITI commitments (Extractive Industries Transparency Initiative, 2017[31]). At the time of writing, civil society is electing its members for the group in an independent manner and according to its own rules. Several civil society organisations have elaborated a code of conduct that sets the criteria for the election process (Lebanese Coalition for Good Governance in Extractive Industries, 2018[32]).

Box 4.3. Code of conduct of civil society organisations involved in EITI

Civil society has become a stakeholder in implementing the EITI since Lebanon announced its intention to join in January 2017.

Civil society actors have therefore devised a code of conduct to help regulate the participation of civil society and define nomination procedures and criteria for the selection of representatives by mutual consent.

It has been formulated in line with the requirements of the EITI standards, which stipulates that "each council from the council of stakeholders shall have the right to appoint its representatives, taking into account the desirability of multiple representation and diversity".

It includes the following sections:

1. Definition of terms, scope and basic principles
2. Rights, duties and obligations of the representative
3. Elections of the members of the stakeholder council
4. Communication practices

Source: Lebanese Coalition for Good Governance in Extractive Industries (2018[32]), Code of Conduct of Civil Society Organisations involved in EITI, https://logi-lebanon.org/KeyIssue/code-of-conduct-process.

Open government literacy and resources

An institutional framework conducive to open government initiatives does not only rely on appropriate co-ordination structures, but also on adequate human resources with the necessary skills. Open government culture is transforming how civil servants work and the skills they require. Engaging in two-way communication, listening to citizens and co-creating public services require skills such as empathy, negotiation and presentation. OECD countries are only at the beginning of their efforts to include these new skills in their public sector workforce. A 2016 OECD report showed that 57% of OECD countries include open government principles in values frameworks, and only 23% include them in competency frameworks, performance agreements and/or accountability frameworks (OECD, 2016[2]). The OECD Recommendation calls for "promoting open government literacy in the administration" and "providing public officials with … adequate human, financial, and technical resources, while promoting a supportive organisational culture". These new interactions with citizens should not be outsourced to contract providers, as meaningful insights come only from the interaction between decision makers and citizens

(OECD, 2017[33]). The OECD Recommendation on Public Service Leadership and Capability therefore provides a framework to highlight the capabilities needed in the public service (see Box 4.4).

Box 4.4. OECD Recommendation on Public Service Leadership and Capability

Adopted in 2019, the 14 principles of the Recommendation aim to identify what makes a public service fit for purpose and responsive today:

1. Defining the values of the public service and promoting values-based decision making.
2. Building leadership capability in the public service.
3. Ensuring an inclusive and safe public service that reflects the diversity of the society it represents.
4. Building a proactive and innovative public service that takes a long-term perspective in the design and implementation of policy and services.
5. Continuously identifying skills and competencies needed to transform political vision into services which deliver value to society.
6. Attracting and retaining employees with the skills and competencies required from the labour market.
7. Recruiting, selecting and promoting candidates through transparent, open and merit-based processes, to guarantee fair and equal treatment.
8. Developing the necessary skills and competencies by creating a learning culture and environment in the public service.
9. Assessing, rewarding and recognising performance, talent and initiative.
10. Clarifying institutional responsibilities for people management to strengthen the effectiveness of the public employment system.
11. Developing a long-term, strategic and systematic approach to people management based on evidence and inclusive planning.
12. Setting the necessary conditions for internal and external workforce mobility and adaptability to match skills with demand.
13. Determining and offering transparent employment terms and conditions (e.g. compensation, term length, job security, rights and obligations) that appropriately match the functions of the position, taking into account external and internal labour markets.
14. Ensuring that employees have opportunities to contribute to the improvement of public service delivery and are engaged as partners in public service management issues.

Source: OECD (2019[34]), *Recommendation of the Council on Public Service Leadership and Capability*, https://legalinstruments.oecd.org/en/instruments/OECD-LEGAL-0445.

A 2017 OECD report, “Skills for a High Performing Civil Service”, provides a framework of the skills needed for service delivery and citizen engagement (OECD, 2017[33]). These skills are:

- **Professional:** Traditional building blocks of service and engagement skills include professionals with expertise in, for example, public relations, communications, marketing, consultation, facilitation, service delivery, conflict resolution, community development and outreach.

- **Strategic:** Using engagement skills to achieve specific outcomes to inform, for example, better targeted interventions, or nudging public behaviour towards desirable outcomes, such as healthier eating habits or smoking reduction.
- **Innovative:** Innovation skills applied to engagement to expand and redesign the tools themselves through, for example, co-creation, prototyping, social media, crowdsourcing, challenge prizes, ethnography, opinion research and data, branding, behavioural insights/nudging, digital service environments, and user data analytics.

Now is a timely moment to introduce the skills required for open government in Lebanon, as the Civil Service Board (CSB) and OMSAR are – at the time of writing – conducting a project on Lebanon's public service, documenting and defining job positions and responsibilities. This is part of a call for restructuring the public sector echoed in the ministerial statement of the 2019 government (Lebanese Forces, 2019[35]). One of the objectives under this restructuring target is to carry out a comprehensive mapping of all government institutions, including staff vacancies and surplus, in order to determine the functional needs of each department. This could be the occasion to introduce the responsibilities and skills related to open government in certain job positions/descriptions. OMSAR is already working on defining the job description and tasks of the official responsible for access to information, a commitment of the national action plan for implementing the Right of Access to Information law, which could serve as good practice to build on.

Introducing these skills in job descriptions and considering them in future hiring processes is however only one approach; training public officials, and thereby enabling them to acquire the required skills, is another approach. This is of particular importance in the current situation, where the 2017 hiring freeze, as foreseen by Law No. 46 dated 21/8/2017, does not allow for the recruitment of further public officials (Division for Sustainable Development Goals, 2018[17]). The existing e-Learning portal currently run by OMSAR, which is envisioned to be transformed into a hub for a national digital academy portal, currently includes courses on, for example, relations with citizens, strategic planning, public employment, management and change management, project management in the digital age, conflict management, and the Covid-19 pandemic response. This portal could be further developed to include a course on open government principles and their application in the public administration. To develop the course OMSAR could partner with international organisations, universities and training institutes such as the Institut des Finances Basil Fuleihan.

Box 4.5. Education in Open Government: A comprehensive and multilevel pedagogical tool by the Spanish government

Education in Open Government is the result of a commitment in the third OGP Spanish National Action Plan 2017–2019. This ongoing initiative has two pedagogical objectives: train students in the development of social and civic competences, specifically the principles of open government, and train teachers for the evaluation of social and civic competences. A third objective goes beyond education and aims to build a civic capacity in youth to fully exercise their democratic rights, demand transparency and accountability to public authorities, and build an active citizenship by giving students the skills and knowledge to be able to interact and participate in the public sphere. Education in Open Government aims to accelerate the open government cultural change by transmitting the principles to those citizens who will be making decisions in the future.

The project started in 2018 led by the Directorate-General of Public Governance, with cross-government co-ordination, and is composed of three levels of action:

1. Training via a massive online open course (MOOC) based on fundamental knowledge about open government and its pillars, as well as the main trends around implementation and outcomes on diverse policy areas. The training targets teachers and the whole education community, as well as any other person interested in open government.
2. The inclusion of open government related content in pedagogical curricula across Spain.
3. Guides of education in open government are pedagogical material for primary, secondary and high school education, and include theoretical and practical knowledge on open government. The guides have been translated into all the official languages of Spain, as well as into English and French.

This project is the first comprehensive educational project specific to open government that takes into account all educational stages and has clear objectives and evaluation mechanisms. This initiative can be replicated for students at university or for civil servants capacity building and in other countries. A pilot project in Latin America and the Caribbean was led by the Spanish Agency for International Development Cooperation.

Sources: OPSI (2018[36]), *Education in Open Government*, https://oecd-opsi.org/innovations/education-in-open-government/; Government of Spain (n.d[37]), Educacion en Gobierno Abierto [Education in Open Government], https://transparencia.gob.es/transparencia/transparencia_Home/index/Gobierno-abierto/EduGobAbierto.html#Componente0; Government of Spain (2017[38]), *Third National Action Plan of Spain 2017-2019 of the Open Government Partnership*, www.opengovpartnership.org/wp-content/uploads/2017/07/Spain_Action-Plan_2017-2019_EN.pdf.

Financing open government initiatives

Responsible institutions require a budget to implement open government initiatives; however, fewer than 20% of OECD countries use the central institution in charge of open government to allocate funds for open government initiatives; however, countries ensure funding through the institutions implementing each project. In some cases, funds are also provided by the European Union (EU) or donors and multilateral organisations (OECD, 2016[2]). Lebanon is currently in a tight fiscal situation with an immense public debt, which led to the CEDRE conference. While the international community has pledged financial support, and some projects such as with the OECD, UNDP and the World Bank exist to financially support specific reform efforts, the government is called upon to develop cost-effective and innovative open government initiatives. Partnerships with civil society, academia and the use of digital tools are therefore advisable.

Recommendations:

- **Formalize the role OMSAR as the leading agency of Lebanon's open government agenda by nominating an open government co-ordinator and defining the responsibilities and tasks of the open government team.** This could be linked to other proposed open government reforms such as developing an action plan and elaborating guidelines for stakeholder participation.
- **Establish a committee on open government, which functions in accordance with existing government committee structures.** This would include coordination and dialogue with the Anti-corruption Ministerial Committee, the Access to Information Committee, and the Ministerial Committee for Digital Economy and Digital Transformation.
- **Introduce responsibilities and skills related to open government in certain job positions/descriptions.** In doing so, develop training courses on open government principles and initiatives, taking advantage of the existing e-learning platform.

References

Canada School of Public Service Digital Academy (2020), *"Busrides" webpage*, https://busrides-trajetsenbus.ca/en/ep-3-en/ (accessed on 2 July 2020). [9]

Division for Sustainable Development Goals (2018), *Lebanon: Voluntary National Review on Sustainable Development Goals*, United Nations, https://sustainabledevelopment.un.org/content/documents/19484Lebanon_VNR_2018.pdf (accessed on 29 October 2019). [19]

Extractive Industries Transparency Initiative (2017), *Lebanon commits to implement EITI*, https://eiti.org/news/lebanon-commits-to-implement-eiti (accessed on 29 October 2019). [14]

Government of Canada (2020), *"Open Government" webpage*, https://open.canada.ca/en (accessed on 2 July 2020). [8]

Government of Canada (n.d.), *Multi-stakeholder Forum Terms of Reference*, https://docs.google.com/document/d/1NHSHqGDQBEuY76d5VA3lcz-AtaMegyUa6C7XE9DKQv0/edit (accessed on 20 November 2019). [6]

Government of Lebanon (2019), *Lebanon Digital Transformation: Strategies to Actions.* [11]

Government of Spain (2017), *Third National Action Plan of Spain 2017-2019 fo the Open Government Partnserhip*, https://www.opengovpartnership.org/wp-content/uploads/2017/07/Spain_Action-Plan_2017-2019_EN.pdf. [22]

Government of Spain (n.d), *Educacion en Gobierno Abierto [Education in Open Government]*, https://transparencia.gob.es/transparencia/transparencia_Home/index/Gobierno-abierto/EduGobAbierto.html#Componente0 (accessed on April 2020). [21]

Lebanese Coalition for Good Governance in Extractive Industries (2018), *Code of Conduct of Civil Society Organisations involved in EITI*, https://logi-lebanon.org/KeyIssue/code-of-conduct-process (accessed on 29 October 2019). [15]

Lebanese Forces (2019), "تفاصيل البيان الوزاري للحكومة الجديدة", https://www.lebanese-forces.com/2019/02/12/new-gov-2/. [18]

May, K. (2018), *"Feds launch 'digital academy' for public service"*, Online article, iPolitics online, https://ipolitics.ca/2018/10/18/feds-launch-new-digital-academy-for-ps-to-help-drive-technology-makeover/ (accessed on 2 July 2020). [10]

OECD (2019), *OECD Recommendation on Digital Government Strategies*, https://www.oecd.org/gov/digital-government/recommendation-on-digital-government-strategies.htm (accessed on 29 October 2019). [13]

OECD (2019), *Open Government in Argentina*, OECD Public Governance Reviews, OECD Publishing, Paris, https://dx.doi.org/10.1787/1988ccef-en. [1]

OECD (2019), *Recommendation of the Council on Public Service Leadership and Capability*, https://legalinstruments.oecd.org/en/instruments/OECD-LEGAL-0445 (accessed on 29 October 2019). [17]

OECD (2017), *Recommendation of the Council on Open Government*, https://legalinstruments.oecd.org/en/instruments/OECD-LEGAL-0438. [12]

OECD (2017), *Skills for a High Performing Civil Service*, OECD Public Governance Reviews, OECD Publishing, Paris, https://dx.doi.org/10.1787/9789264280724-en. [16]

OECD (2016), *Open Government in Tunisia*, OECD Public Governance Reviews, OECD Publishing, Paris, https://dx.doi.org/10.1787/9789264227118-en. [3]

OECD (2016), *Open Government: The Global Context and the Way Forward*, OECD Publishing, Paris, https://dx.doi.org/10.1787/9789264268104-en. [2]

OGP (2019), *OGP Handbook Rules and Guidance for Participants*, Open Government Partnership, https://www.opengovpartnership.org/wp-content/uploads/2019/03/OGP_Handbook-Rules-Guidance-for-Participants_20190313.pdf (accessed on 15 November 2019). [4]

OGP (2018), *OGP Participation and Co-Creation Toolkit*, Open Government Partnership, https://www.opengovpartnership.org/stories/ogps-participation-and-co-creation-toolkit-from-usual-suspects-to-business-as-usual/ (accessed on 15 November 2019). [5]

OPSI (2018), *Education in Open Government*, Observatory of Public Sector Innovation, https://oecd-opsi.org/innovations/education-in-open-government/ (accessed on 3 April 2020). [20]

Treasury Board of Canada Secretariat (n.d.), *"Open Government Team: Work packages"*, unpublished draft. [7]

Chapter 5. Monitoring and evaluation framework

Designing and implementing open government initiatives requires resources and changes in the public administration. While these initiatives are intended to improve the relationship between government and its citizens, as well as enhance transparency and accountability, this can only be ensured and confirmed, and therefore the use of funds and efforts justified, through effective monitoring and evaluation (M&E) systems. A solid M&E system is necessary for assessing if intended goals are achieved, for identifying challenges and obstacles, and for rectifying initiatives accordingly.

Defining Monitoring and Evaluation:

Monitoring refers to "a continuing function that uses systematic collection of data on specified indicators to provide management and the main stakeholders of an ongoing [...] intervention with indications of the extent of progress and achievement of objectives and progress in the use of allocated funds" (OECD, 2009[39]). Therefore, it aims to ensure that the initiative is on track and that it is achieving the intended results, enabling initiatives to be to modified and adapted if necessary.

Evaluation refers to "the systematic and objective assessment of an ongoing or completed project, programme or policy, its design, implementation and results. The aim is to determine the relevance and fulfilment of objectives, [...] efficiency, effectiveness, impact and sustainability" (OECD, 2009[39]). Thus, it allows for the cost-effectiveness of an initiative to be measured, provides information to those implementing policy, as well as the larger public, on whether the initiative is achieving its intended impact, and allows for future initiatives to be enhanced.

M&E systems can therefore enhance the implementation of open government initiatives, and increase their visibility and impact. This requires, however, closing the feedback loop and using the M&E results to improve ongoing and future initiatives. In line with open government principles, M&E results should be made available to the public to enhance accountability and enable citizens to scrutinise government actions. Similarly, the public should be involved in M&E systems, especially as most open government initiatives intend to affect citizens and their perception of government directly.

A large majority of OECD countries (86%) monitor open government initiatives, yet only 59% evaluate these initiatives. Almost all countries that evaluate initiatives communicate the results. However, most countries have not put in place specific M&E systems regarding open government (except those required by the OGP), but are building upon the existing M&E frameworks of their public administration (OECD, 2016[2]). The OECD Recommendation on Open Government therefore suggests that countries:

"Develop and implement monitoring, evaluation and learning mechanisms for open government strategies and initiatives by:

1. Identifying institutional actors to be in charge of collecting and disseminating up-to-date and reliable information and data in an open format.

2. Developing comparable indicators to measure processes, outputs, outcomes and impact in collaboration with stakeholders.
3. Fostering a culture of monitoring, evaluation and learning among public officials by increasing their capacity to regularly conduct exercises for these purposes in collaboration with relevant stakeholders." (OECD, 2017[1])

Box 5.1. Monitoring and evaluation of open government initiatives in OECD member and partner countries

One of the great challenges OECD member and partner countries currently face in the area of open government is to move the focus from processes to outcomes and impact (OECD, 2019[40]). The implementation of open government strategies usually involves initiatives in a variety of areas and requires the involvement of multiple stakeholders. Given this multidimensional and cross-cutting nature, open government initiatives are difficult to monitor and evaluate. However, solid monitoring and evaluation (M&E) mechanisms can help to ensure that policies are achieving the intended goals, contribute to the identification of policy design and implementation barriers, and orient policy choices by building on past experiences (OECD, 2019[40]). M&E is also instrumental to initiating changes and communicating policy results in a timely and accessible manner. Examples from OECD member and partner countries include:

Spain has established a dashboard for monitoring its third open government action plan. The progress made is updated every three months in all the available categories, including axis, commitment and category. Stakeholders can also provide comments through a questionnaire available for each commitment. The dashboard provides detailed information on progress, including briefing notes, outcomes, dates for each activity, and the state of implementation of each activity. A general summary is provided with the progress made on the overall plan. This dashboard provides valuable data to monitor the implementation of the plan.

Mexico's open government metrics were developed by the Centre for Economic Research and Teaching (CIDE) and based on an initiative of the National Institute for Transparency, Access to Information and Personal Data Protection (INAI). The metrics are designed as a baseline to measure the current state of the National System of Transparency, Access to Information and Protection of Personal Data (SNT) and its open government and transparency policies. Aiming to be an "x-ray of the starting point of the open government policy of the Mexican State" at the national and subnational level, its focus goes beyond measuring compliance with regulations and aims to capture performance information on the outcomes of open government and transparency policies from the perspective of both government and citizens. The metrics start with an operational definition of open government that is structured around two dimensions: transparency and public participation. Each dimension is then approached from two perspectives: government and citizens. The metrics survey included a sample of 908 governmental bodies at the national and subnational level; 754 portals were reviewed and 3 635 requests for information were sent. The resulting Open Government Index of Mexico was 0.39 (on a scale of 0 to 1). The index showed that the transparency dimension had a much higher value (0.50) than the participation dimension (0.28).

Argentina has integrated the monitoring and evaluation of its open government initiatives into the wider framework provided by the State Modernisation Plan (adopted in 2016). Under the leadership of the Office of the Chief of Cabinet of Ministers, the Government Secretariat of Modernisation has developed an integral system to standardise planning, monitoring and evaluation in co-operation with all line ministries. This system contains several dashboards to monitor the progress on open government initiatives, namely the Results Management Dashboard (*Tablero de Gestión por Resultados*), the Integral Management Dashboard (*Tablero de Gestión Integral*) and the Strategic Monthly Report (*Informe Mensual Estratégico*). With these tools, the public can track the development and implementation of key open government initiatives, such as the follow-up of the third OGP Action Plan. In addition, to offer citizens the possibility of assessing efforts in implementing priority projects, a Citizen's Dashboard was launched in 2018. The five key areas that the dashboard covers are open government, public employment, digital government, digital inclusion and connectivity. It includes information on 20 different projects and provides information on their content, impact and progress, with process and output indicators.

Sources: OECD (2019[6]), *Open Government in Argentina*, OECD Public Governance Reviews, https://doi.org/10.1787/1988ccef-en; OECD (2019[41]), *Open Government in Biscay*, OECD Public Governance Reviews, https://doi.org/10.1787/e4e1a40c-en; Datos.gob (2020[42]), "Open Data Initiative of the Government of Spain", https://datos.gob.es/en.

Lebanon has established an M&E system in the public administration that builds on internal monitoring and M&E conducted by an external institution, namely the Central Inspection Board (CIB). The internal monitoring system is based on key performance indicators (KPIs) and sub-KPIs, as is used for the digital transformation strategy and the action plan for implementing the Right of Access to Information law. Some of these KPIs refer to open government indicators such as "inclusive citizen/customer-oriented policy making", according to the OECD survey. Table 5.1. shows the KPIs prepared for "citizens centricity" in the framework of the draft Digital Transformation Strategy.

Table 5.1. Extract from the draft key performance areas and sub-areas of the draft Digital Transformation Strategy

Key performance area: Citizens Centricity

Citizen experience with government services	Measure and monitor the level of citizen satisfaction with their experience using the government services.
Online availability of citizen services	Assess the availability of citizen digital services online 24x365
Tell us once, not often	Citizens should provide information only once and must not be requested to enter the same information time and time again.
Citizen participation and engagement	Measure and monitor the level of citizen participation and engagement in digital transformation projects and services.
Quality of citizen online interactions	Assess and monitor the quality of citizen interactions with the offered government digital services.
Citizen channel shift to digital services	Monitor the volume of citizen transactions shifted from traditional channels to digital service channels.
Citizen access to information	Assure easy unhindered access for citizens to needed information.
Data governance and classification	Data must be classified properly so that they can be protected. Access is governed based on pre-established classification criteria.
Transparency and accountability	Citizens must have access to government digital services in a transparent and predictable manner.
Consistency in obtaining citizen services	Monitor the consistency in obtaining citizen services to ensure transparency and fairness.

Source: Government of Lebanon (2019[8]), *Lebanon Digital Transformation: Strategies to Actions*.

OMSAR is supporting the public administration in applying these KPIs and in building the capacities of public officials and inspectors. It is also automating the methodology through the development of a web-based solution, which should facilitate reporting to the CIB. OMSAR also intends to create sectoral and organisational performance planning and monitoring units in all institutions. However, the public administration still faces challenges in monitoring its activities due to insufficient expertise and resources in the field. There is equally a lack of reliable data, the publication of results could become a more common feature and engaging citizens in the process is rare. The OECD survey found that OMSAR conducted citizen satisfaction surveys on e-government services in 2013 and surveys to prioritise digital transformation projects in 2019. This is a practice other institutions could build on, and the results should be made publicly available. Given OMSAR's role regarding open government and supporting the public administration on M&E, OMSAR could work with those ministries that are to be involved in the open government sub-committee on building an M&E culture, expertise and indicators for the open government initiatives included in the open government action plan. The existing e-learning platform (see Chapter 4) could be complemented with a course on M&E focusing in particular on the M&E of open government initiatives and stakeholder engagement in M&E.

As per legislative decree 111/1959, all directors-general should submit biannual and annual reports to central control agencies (Article 7, item 4). According to Circular 40/1963, the CIB issued instructions on the conduct of inspection processes for public sector entities. OMSAR, together with the CIB, is currently enforcing this with six pilot ministries. The OECD survey found that one of the KPIs that should be included in these reports relates to open government. In order to strengthen the M&E of open government initiatives, OMSAR and the CIB could enhance their expertise in this field and develop specific indicators that build upon the existing KPIs and that evaluate the process, output, outcome and impact of open government initiatives. Such a pilot project could focus on the open government initiatives to be included in the open government action plan.

Figure 5.1. Examples of indicators associated with an open government initiative

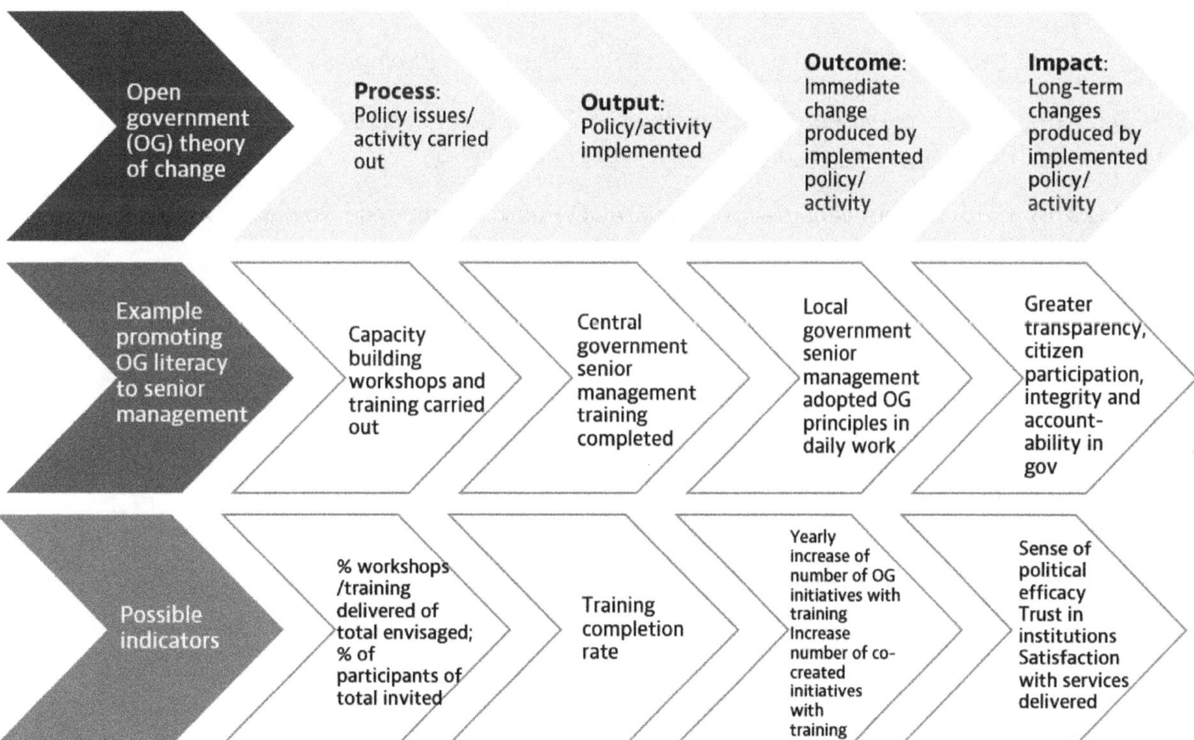

Source: OECD (2019[6]), *Open Government in Argentina*, https://dx.doi.org/10.1787/1988ccef-en.

According to interviews with the CIB and other actors, vacancies among inspectors does not allow the CIB to effectively practice control mechanisms over the public administration. While it is important to reinforce their capacities, involving stakeholders in M&E could also support a more effective monitoring and evaluation of open government initiatives. In several OECD countries, civil society organisations are members of the open government steering committee, which enables them to monitor the implementation of initiatives.

Recommendations:

- **Continue efforts to strengthen Lebanon's M&E system by automating the process and providing capacity building for the public administration.**
- **Apply open government principles to the M&E system by systematically engaging with all relevant stakeholders and publishing the results of M&E, including the results of the different institutions and the CIB.**
- **Build an M&E culture and system regarding open government initiatives by developing indicators for the open government initiatives**. These could then be included in the future open government action plan and complemented by an M&E learning course with a focus on open government and stakeholder engagement.

References

Datos.gob (2020), *Open Data Initiative of the Government of Spain*, https://datos.gob.es/en (accessed on 29 June 2020). [7]

Government of Lebanon (2019), *Lebanon Digital Transformation: Strategies to Actions*. [8]

OECD (2019), *Budgeting and Public Expenditures in OECD Countries 2019*, OECD Publishing, Paris, https://dx.doi.org/10.1787/9789264307957-en. [4]

OECD (2019), *Open Government in Argentina*, OECD Public Governance Reviews, OECD Publishing, Paris, https://dx.doi.org/10.1787/1988ccef-en. [5]

OECD (2019), *Open Government in Biscay*, OECD Public Governance Reviews, OECD Publishing, Paris, https://dx.doi.org/10.1787/e4e1a40c-en. [6]

OECD (2017), *Recommendation of the Council on Open Government*, https://legalinstruments.oecd.org/en/instruments/OECD-LEGAL-0438. [3]

OECD (2016), *Open Government: The Global Context and the Way Forward*, OECD Publishing, Paris, https://dx.doi.org/10.1787/9789264268104-en. [2]

OECD (2009), "OECD DAC Glossary", in *Guidelines for Project and Programme Evaluations*, OECD, Paris, http://www.oecd.org/development/evaluation/dcdndep/47069197.pdf (accessed on 29 October 2019). [1]

Chapter 6. Communication and information

Public communication as an essential part of open government initiatives

Public communication is a means for governments to inform and interact with citizens. It enables citizens to be informed about policies and reforms that affect their lives and become engaged in policy-making processes. "When delivered strategically public communication can support better policy making and service delivery, as it raises awareness about reforms and helps to change behaviour." (OECD, 2019[6]) Communication is therefore an essential part of open government initiatives as it can promote greater transparency, participation and accountability. Provision 6 of the OECD Recommendation on Open Government calls upon adherents to "actively communicate on open government strategies and initiatives, as well as on their outputs, outcomes and impacts, in order to ensure that they are well-known within and outside government, to favour their uptake, as well as to stimulate stakeholder buy-in" (OECD, 2017[1]). However, the importance of public communication is still not fully recognised; for example, only 10% of surveyed centres of government list the promotion of transparency and stakeholder participation as a key objective of their communication strategy (OECD, 2018[43]).

Strategic communication can be characterised as a driver of more effective communication. It is typically planned and co-ordinated at senior management levels within specialised units. Strategic communication structures have defined functions that enable an integrated and organised communication activity, which facilitate greater stakeholder engagement to help shape organisational goals. Such activities are undertaken by skilled professionals who occupy positions at various levels of organisational charts. Mechanisms to assess the effectiveness of communication activities with measurable outcomes are also envisioned under strategic communication activities, together with the employment of digital technologies to facilitate stakeholder engagement.

Communication and information efforts in Lebanon

Lebanon has not introduced reforms for public communication or set out an overall vision that aims to promote effective communication between the government and the public. However, in the framework of the ongoing open government reforms, OMSAR and the Prime Minister's Office have been working to integrate communication and information practices more strategically.

Few institutional communication structures exist

In Lebanon, the organisational charts of most ministries and public institutions do not include a dedicated unit for communications, and administrations in the country do not have public communication officers nor communication units within their agencies. Such functions remain centralised and managed by senior leadership: For instance, ministers are the official spokespeople and communications activities need to be cleared by the minister first.[1]

Most ministers hire media advisors when they take office, with the exception of a few ministries and public institutions, such as the Ministry of Social Affairs and the Institute of Finance, which have media units. These media advisors are most often political appointees who do not fall under the permanent civil servant category. Budgets for communication activities are either very limited or do not exist at all. Alternatively, some ministries hire communication officers for donor-funded projects, who also cover the activities of the ministry. Another common pattern observed in ministries is the assignment of communication functions to either information technology personnel or employees in charge of e-services units.[2]

Scarce funding deters stability and continuity in the planning of communication functions. As a result, specialised training for skills development in communications has not been conducted so far for public sector employees. As public communication is not institutionalised, no legislations or policies have been developed to regulate this area. The main roles of media and communication advisors, commonly recruited by ministers, are mainly restricted to media relations and media campaigns. Such roles remain limited to developing messaging and do not include citizen insight research for engagement.

As highlighted in Chapter 4, the ongoing mapping exercise by OMSAR and the Civil Service Board to outline the organisational charts that need to be amended and to assess the administrative needs of each public entity[3] could be an opportunity to introduce public communication structures and functions in the public administration. For most public institutions in the country, organisational charts have not been reviewed since their establishment. Breakthroughs in information and communication technology (ICT) have increased pressure on administrations to become more agile and citizen-centric. In light of these continuous ICT changes, administrations are expected to continue the cycles of reflection and reorganisation. As communication channels and objectives have become more complex with the development of social media and citizen engagement targets, organisational structures have become more specialised in various countries (Sanders and Canel, 2013[44]). For example, the United Kingdom has developed a Government Communication Service (GCS), which is one of 14 functions that operate across the civil service to bring together over 4 000 professionals across 25 ministerial departments (UK Government, 2019[45]). GCS staff are in charge of implementing campaigns, evaluating their outcomes, using technology to gain audience insights and promoting internal communication amongst government agencies (UK Government, 2019[45]).

As mentioned, the ongoing review of organisational charts of the whole administration in Lebanon provides a great opportunity to institutionalise public communication across the government. The redesign could introduce communication units across ministerial departments and public entities to create the institutional structure for outreach activities and greater internal co-ordination within the administration. Regarding open government initiatives, the structures, and particularly the communication officers, play an important role. Therefore, their capacity and awareness of transparency and two-way communication should be fostered through capacity building activities and guidelines.

The use of social media is of particular importance in this context. With 78% of the Lebanese population on Facebook (Mideastmedia.org, 2020[46]), the use of social media could become a widespread tool to proactively inform citizens. Its ability to allow users to engage in a two-way conversation can further enhance open government principles; however, social media also bears risks related to hate speech and disinformation. Accordingly, governments are encouraged to put in place policies and guidelines for the use of social media in public communication. OMSAR has taken the first steps in setting-up communication in favour of open government through its Twitter account (@OmsarGov) and the corresponding hashtags (#OpenGov or #OpenGovLeb), as well as its Facebook account. Integrating these communication efforts strategically into the open government agenda, and providing training and guidelines on the effective use of social media, could contribute to greater transparency and dialogue.

Current information and communication efforts regarding open government initiatives

The proactive disclosure of information, which is foreseen by Lebanon's Right of Access to Information Law (see Chapter 3), is another critical aspect to using communication to enhance open government. The effective communication and disclosure of government and public administration information depends, however, on the policies in place. The OECD Recommendation suggests that countries should "proactively make available clear, complete, timely, reliable and relevant public sector data and information that is free of cost, available in an open and non-proprietary machine-readable format, easy to find, understand, use and reuse, and disseminated through a multi-channel approach, to be prioritised in consultation with stakeholders" (OECD, 2017[1]).

Lebanon has undertaken some efforts in this regard, including the development of a Public Sector Projects and Studies department within OMSAR, which is responsible for consolidating all studies generated from the public sector either directly or through consultants and consulting firms. These studies are classified and indexed in a database that is accessible online for researchers, scholars and interested individuals. Despite these efforts, some major impediments still exist, including the cost of accessing the official gazette, which is where Parliament publishes adopted laws (as described in Chapter 8). To enhance transparency, Lebanon could consider making the official gazette freely available. OMSAR, in the framework of the draft Digital Transformation Strategy, is also undertaking efforts regarding proactive disclosure. Under Action 9 of the strategy, the government vows to establish an open data platform, www.data.gov.lb, that will enable government entities to publish high-quality open datasets. The government also promises to develop a platform, www.lebanon.gov.lb, that will be devoted to the publication of government information in order to enhance citizens' access to information (Government of Lebanon, 2019[8]). In line with these efforts, an e-procurement portal is also under development and will soon be launched once the necessary legal framework is operationalised. The digitalisation of the administration and building the necessary skills are preconditions to render these portals effective.

The Central Administration for Statistics (CAS) could play a significant role in ensuring that public entities become more transparent and provide citizens with evidence-based information to promote a well-informed public debate. CAS is a public administration that falls under the presidency of the Council of Ministers. Its mission is to collect, produce and disseminate social and economic statistics, as well as to conduct technical supervision of statistics produced by other ministries to harmonise methods. CAS is also responsible for gathering the datasets of all public administrations, and each ministry should send all its datasets to CAS for archiving every three months. More recently, CAS has started producing time series, with 11 time series databases currently regularly updated on its website. However, it does not have a media or communications department, nor a strategy to increase traffic to its website. In addition, a lot of the data are not in open formats (mostly PDF format), which goes against the principle of open data that aims to facilitate re-use.

Budget transparency

A major policy document that provides information about the government's priorities and actions is the budget. Lebanon did not adopt a budget law between 1997 and 2016, with the first budget law being adopted again in 2017. The Ministry of Finance has undertaken an enormous effort to reconstruct all budgets, which were sent to the Court of Audit (which is suffering from staff shortages) for auditing and to Parliament to close the budgets. These budgets have however not yet been audited nor closed and are not accessible to the public. The only budget that has been audited is the one from 2017; however, this was neither discussed in Parliament nor made available to the public. Encouraging the publication of these documents would greatly enhance transparency and enable citizens to oversee government actions.

The Ministry of Finance, with the support of the Institute of Finance, has undertaken efforts to strengthen budget transparency by publishing the adopted Budget Law and producing citizen budgets for 2018-2020.

While a citizen budget is recognised internationally as a means to facilitate citizen's understanding of the state budget, civil society's ability to play a watchdog function and be adequately informed about the government's policies would be enhanced if the budget were published in an open data format (in the long-term also on the open data platform) and included explanations about budget choices and their objectives. In line with best practice and the International Budget Partnership standards, the Ministry of Finance could consider publishing the draft budget before it is formally approved by Parliament.

Recommendations:

- **Create public communication structures, officials and a network that unites communicators across the administration.** In doing so, provide them with training on information and communication practices regarding open government and the use of social media.
- **Consider making the official gazette freely available to enhance transparency.**
- **Advance efforts to digitalise the administration and make public information readily available in an open, easily accessible, interoperable and re-usable format on the planned online portals (www.data.gov.lb and www.lebanon.gov.lb).**
- **Adopt international practices regarding budget transparency by publishing the draft budget law, the audit report and the budget law in an open data format.**

Notes

[1] Information collected during the peer review missions in September 2019.

[2] Information collected during the peer review missions in September 2019.

[3] Information collected during the peer review missions in September 2019.

References

Government of Lebanon (2019), *Lebanon Digital Transformation: Strategies to Actions*. [7]

Mideastmedia.org (2020), *"Social Media: Use by Platform" webpage*, http://www.mideastmedia.org/survey/2017/chapter/social-media/ (accessed on 2 July 2020). [6]

OECD (2019), *Open Government in Argentina*, OECD Public Governance Reviews, OECD Publishing, Paris, https://dx.doi.org/10.1787/1988ccef-en. [1]

OECD (2018), *Centre Stage 2: The Organisation and Functions of the Centre of Government in OECD Countries*, http://www.oecd.org/gov/centre-stage-2.pdf (accessed on 29 October 2019). [3]

OECD (2017), *Recommendation of the Council on Open Government*, https://legalinstruments.oecd.org/en/instruments/OECD-LEGAL-0438. [2]

Sanders, K. and M. Canel (2013), *Government communication in 15 countries: Themes and* [4] *challenges*, https://www.ucm.es/data/cont/media/www/pag-37870/Government%20communication%20in%2015%20countries-1.%20Themes%20and%20challenges.pdf.

UK Government (2019), *Government Communication Plan 2019/2020*, https://gcs.civilservice.gov.uk/communication-plan-2019/wp-content/uploads/2019/04/Government-Communication-Plan-2019.pdf. [5]

Chapter 7. Participation practices and innovation

OECD principles

One of the core principles of an open government culture is stakeholder participation. This refers to all the ways in which stakeholders can be involved in the policy cycle and in service design and delivery and can include different levels of participation, including:

- **Information**: An initial level of participation characterised by a one-way relationship in which the government produces and delivers information to stakeholders. It covers both the on-demand provision of information and "proactive" measures by the government to disseminate information.
- **Consultation**: A more advanced level of participation that entails a two-way relationship in which stakeholders provide feedback to the government and vice versa. It is based on the prior definition of the issue for which views are being sought and requires the provision of relevant information, in addition to feedback on the outcomes of the process.
- **Engagement**: When stakeholders are given the opportunity and the necessary resources (e.g. information, data and digital tools) to collaborate during all phases of the policy cycle and in service design and delivery (OECD, 2017[1]).

The reasons for governments adopting participatory approaches and the objectives they aim to achieve vary, but generally include instrumental benefits, which refers to creating better results such as an improved policy, law or service; and intrinsic benefits, which refers to an improved process that is more legitimate, transparent, accountable, and inclusive, and that thereby contributes to building trust, strengthening social cohesion and enhancing representative democracy (OECD, 2016[2]). In this sense, the OECD Recommendation on Open Government affirms "that stakeholder participation increases government accountability, broadens citizens' empowerment and influence on decisions, builds civic capacity, improves the evidence base for policy making, reduces implementation costs, and taps wider networks for innovation in policy making and service delivery" (OECD, 2017[1]).

Box 7.1. Benefits of consultation

- **Transparency and access to information**: Public consultation can increase the transparency of the rule-making process because stakeholders have access to the process itself, as well as to timely and relevant information about the proposed legislation. Consultation therefore contributes to equal access to information.
- **Added value**: The public is a rich source of instant and updated information. It is the driver of innovation, and public consultation enables policy makers to make use of the public's precious experience and knowledge.
- **Alienation and connectivity**: Public engagement in rule making can raise support for regulations as citizens feel connected to the policy-making process. Disenchantment with politics runs the risk of declining support for reform and of undermining public confidence and trust in national political institutions.
- **Increased compliance**: Engaging the public and striving for consensus can help to increase the social acceptance of regulations. It can contribute to greater compliance and therefore reduce enforcement costs.
- **Regulatory literacy**: Stakeholders will learn about the complexities of setting regulations, finding compromises and trade-offs. Open government illustrates to the public the constraints and limitations faced by authorities. Public consultation therefore promotes public education on rule making and provides stakeholders with a chance to increase their regulatory literacy.
- **Anticipating the impact**: Public consultation is necessary to anticipate the likely impact of the regulation on stakeholders, contemplate unintended consequences, and consider alternatives to the proposed regulatory option.
- **Managing conflict**: Public consultation provides a mechanism to manage conflicts at an early stage. Engaging the public in rule making is one tool for mediating various interests in society and increasing awareness of compromises.
- **Pursued public interest**: Quality regulations are based on public interest. However, public interest is not static, but a dynamic concept that needs to be continuously defined. The definition and pursuit of public interest can only take place through a dialogue with the public.

Source: OECD (2012[47]), Regulatory Consultation: A MENA-OECD practitioners' guide for engaging stakeholders in the rule-making process, www.oecd.org/mena/governance/MENA-Practitioners-Guide-%20EN.pdf.

The objectives to be achieved through adopting participatory approaches vary according to when in the policy-cycle stakeholders are engaged. As Figure 7.1shows, stakeholders could be involved at several stages ranging from the definition of priorities to the evaluation of the policy. Data from OECD countries show, however, that governments most often open the policy cycle to input at the phase of drafting a policy and when seeking feedback on a policy or service (OECD, 2016[2]).

Figure 7.1. Policy cycle

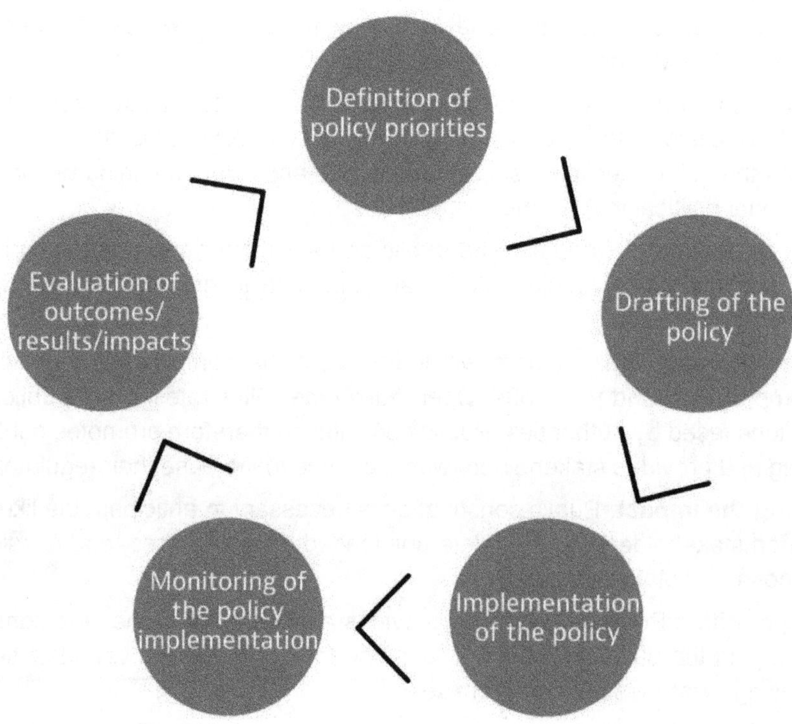

Source: OECD (2016[2]), *Open Government: The Global Context and the Way Forward*, https://dx.doi.org/10.1787/9789264268104-en.

Finally, and in line with the three levels of participation, governments have a variety of tools and means to engage stakeholders. The appropriate choice of the engagement tool depends on the objectives to be achieved, the question at hand and the stakeholders to be involved. In most cases, a mix of several tools is most appropriate in order to receive diverse input and to ensure that citizens can participate in their preferred way. Box 7.2 highlights a set of tools available. Further examples can also be found on the OECD Open Government Toolkit Navigator.[1]

Box 7.2. Participatory tools

There are a wide variety of participatory tools available to governments that can enhance information, consultation and the engagement of stakeholders. A combination of several tools is most likely to achieve an inclusive approach to participation as it enables stakeholders to participate in their preferred ways. Some examples include:

Citizen newsletters: This is an information tool mostly shared by email to which citizens can subscribe if they are interested in receiving regular updates on policies, events and participation opportunities. The cities of Barcelona and Paris offer such a tool.

Online consultation and idea suggestion platforms: Such online consultation tools offer a variety of opportunities for citizens to participate. This can include the publication of policies or laws for an online consultation, as well as an "idea box" where citizens can proactively provide ideas for new policies or laws. Some open-source platforms are available, such as "Consul" used by the city of Madrid.

Town hall meeting: This is an opportunity for citizens and the government to dialogue. It is often a physical meeting where citizens can question the government on specific topics or discuss a specific policy.

Participatory budgeting: This was first used in Brazil as an engagement tool. The objective is to enable citizens to decide upon the spending of a specific percentage of the investment budget. Several hundred cities around the world apply this tool, and the government of Portugal applies it at the national level. Generally, the process includes several stages: idea suggestion where citizens propose projects, an assessment of these proposals by the government (assessing feasibility), and a voting stage where citizens decide which projects will be implemented.

Advisory councils: These "are composed of representatives of public interest, who are appointed by government bodies, with the aim of ensuring broad representation and providing a forum for ongoing consultation". They are mostly thematic focused, such as youth councils or elderly councils.

Citizen assembly: Citizens are randomly selected and usually meet over several days or weeks to deliberate a specific policy issue. They receive input and ideas from a selection of experts to enable an informed decision-making process. The assembly's recommendations can be put up for a referendum, parliamentary debate or be the basis of government policy. Ireland has used this approach on abortion and France on climate policy.

Hackathons: These are a co-creation tool based on collaborative computer programming. They often involve engaging stakeholders to find innovative solutions to societal issues. The government of France, for example, organised a Hackathon based on the data collected through the *Grand Débat*.

Source: Author's own creation; OECD (2001[48]), *Citizens as Partners: OECD Handbook on Information, Consultation and Public Participation in Policy-Making*, https://doi.org/10.1787/9789264195578-en; and Participedia (2020[49]), "Methods" webpage, https://participedia.net/?selectedCategory=method.

Participatory practices in Lebanon

Lebanon has committed to open government reforms and to engaging citizens and other stakeholders in the policy cycle. As noted in Chapter 3, Circular No. 21/2012 of 25 August 2012 requires all public entities to publish draft legal texts on government websites and solicit consultation and feedback from stakeholders, including civil society. Public entities are required by this circular to assess the feedback received from consultation and integrate it as necessary into updated versions of the legal texts. Similarly, work completed under Afkar III includes the establishment of a policy dialogue platform and detailed guidance, with several pilots implemented. These efforts are implemented in a challenging environment, which is characterised, according to the OECD survey, by distrust between government and civil society and a still too widespread culture of secrecy, for example cabinet meetings and parliamentary sessions are held behind closed doors. Despite this situation, Lebanon can build on several positive experiences in engaging stakeholders that have resulted in more trusting relationships between the ministries and civil society organisations concerned.

Notably, these positive experiences include the process of drafting the national anti-corruption strategy. The Technical Anti-corruption Committee, which is made up of several state institutions, led the work and consulted with various stakeholders, including parliament, civil society, the private sector and trade unions, as well as with the UNDP Regional Project on Anti-corruption and Integrity in the Arab Region. The strategy includes as its sixth outcome "enhancing the participation of society in promoting a culture of integrity" through awareness and educational programmes targeting the wider public, and encouraging non-governmental organisations (NGOs) to play a role in particular "in all aspects of the national strategy: preparation of public policies and strategies, proposals of projects and laws, monitoring and evaluation of public affairs and public administrations". This also includes strengthening journalists' capacity to support the fight against corruption. Similarly, the elaboration of the national action plan for the implementation of the Right of Access to Information Law saw the active participation of civil society, media and academics in the drafting process, and their involvement in the implementation is equally foreseen (see Chapter 3).

As has been undertaken in countries such as Costa Rica (OECD, 2016[2]), Lebanese civil society could consider creating a network of civil society organisations focused on open government and its principles. The network could bring together stakeholders involved in the promotion of different elements of Lebanon's open government agenda, including those advocating for EITI and OGP membership, as well as civil society organisations working in the fields of access to information, open data and anti-corruption. Such a network could allow for a more structured approach to open government and ensure the inclusiveness and representativeness of civil society voices. The network could also play a key role in promoting open government principles and practices at the local level.

Lebanon could build on these positive examples to establish more regular and institutionalised engagement with civil society actors in the field of public governance and open government, more specifically an open government stakeholder network. Such a co-ordination mechanism can help to engage other state actors, such as Parliament and local administrations, as well as actors from society, such as academia, civil society, media and the private sector. This forum could build upon the experiences of the national committee formed in 2017 to oversee the implementation of the Sustainable Development Goals (SDGs), and should interact with these goals. The committee is chaired by the prime minister and includes more than 50 state officials, as well as two representatives from the private sector and two from civil society, namely the Hariri Foundation for Sustainable Human Development and Caritas Lebanon. It is a co-ordinating body for the SDGs and is responsible for raising awareness about the goals and ensuring that they are integrated into national policies and programmes. The committee presents a way of institutionally involving civil society in the SDG process. While it only includes two large organisations, these organisations conducted a series of national consultations and workshops with more than 300 civil society representatives. The committee has several working groups, including a thematic group on peace, led by OMSAR, which is responsible for the implementation of SDG 16 on peace, justice and strong institutions (Division for Sustainable Development Goals, 2018[17]). As SDG 16 calls for the implementation of open government principles, this thematic group should be involved in any co-ordination or consultation mechanism set up for open government reforms.

The public consultation conducted by the Lebanese Petroleum Association is another consultative process that can be seen as inspiration for further participatory approaches. In line with the legal requirements, the Lebanese government commissioned a Strategic Environmental Assessment (SEA) for the Exploration and Production Activities Offshore Lebanon in 2011, which was published in 2014. As the first assessment relied on limited consultation with different ministries and provided for no involvement of civil society (Lebanese Oil and Gas Initiative, 2017[50]), the Lebanese Petroleum Association, following civil society advocacy, organised a public consultation in 2019. The public was able to submit written comments during a period of seven weeks on the draft SEA. This online consultation was complemented by five public consultation sessions in Beirut, Tripoli, Byblos, Saida and Naqoura (Lebanese Petroleum Administration, 2019[51]). The revised SEA has not yet been published at the time of writing.

These examples could provide a basis to elaborate the suggested guidelines on stakeholder engagement (see Chapter 3) in order to further institutionalise consultative and participatory approaches in policy making.

Using e-democracy tools

The draft Digital Transformation Strategy and its related action plan also puts an important emphasis on stakeholder participation, and notes that most governmental entities currently do not engage citizens in the design of their digital services. The strategy therefore aims to encourage the public administration to engage with citizens and get their feedback through a variety of different digital platforms and traditional methods such as events, town hall meetings and conferences. Citizens and other stakeholders should be consulted in the design and rollout of different services and regarding the development of new technologies such as blockchain and artificial intelligence. As Box 7.3 shows, the action plan foresees an awareness campaign for citizens and the development of e-participation tools. In order to measure success, the key performance indicators include citizen and business participation.

The use of e-democracy tools is a common feature in OECD countries; however, their success depends on the uptake of these initiatives by citizens. Reaching a diverse audience is often a challenge, as can be the back office and feedback loops needed to ensure that stakeholders receive information on how their input was used or why it was not taken into account. Lebanon could therefore consider adopting an inclusive and collaborative process that includes stakeholders inside and outside the public administration in the design and roll-out of the e-participation platform. The government should equally consider combining these efforts with offline participation opportunities.

Box 7.3. Extracts from Lebanon's draft Digital Transformation Strategy

Under the pillar "people", the strategy foresees developing, among others, the following two actions:

Citizen awareness campaign

These are the suggested tools and activities:

- One national campaign that reinforces the trust of citizens in the government as a modern, beneficiary-centric public authority that provides high-quality e-services to its citizens professionally and efficiently.
- Public service announcements, e.g. educational awareness videos, posters and billboards.
- Annual surveys to measure citizen satisfaction with the services that government entities offer.
- Social media engagement to reach out to the youth and next generation of citizens.
- An interactive, modern, updated and mobile-responsive unified portal.
- Media and press engagement.
- Awareness sessions in schools, universities, professional organisations, trade unions and NGOs.
- Online mechanisms, such as issue tracking systems (ITS), provided for citizen feedback and exchange.

E-participation

Below are suggested initiatives for e-participation:

- Establish a platform for e-participation.
- Launch an information campaign and advertise in several media, such as social media and newspapers. Provide education on several issues, such as eServices and how to use them, the benefits of digital transformation, and security. Social media campaigns include like/dislike or quick surveys.
- Establish a digital transformation website and social media to inform the public about issues related to the digital transformation.
- Create incentives for using e-services and encourage feedback by having prizes, competitions and special features.

Source: Government of Lebanon (2019[8]), *Lebanon Digital Transformation: Strategies to Actions*.

Inclusive legislative processes

In some cases, civil society associations have drafted laws and bills on crucial matters and presented them to the concerned authority and/or institution, including the Right of Access to Information Law. To further encourage stakeholder participation in the legislative process, Lebanon could consider including a dedicated section in the planned e-participation platform for the consultation process of draft laws. As noted above, the legal framework is supported by Circular No. 21/2012, which requires all public entities to publish draft legal texts on government websites for at least 15 days to solicit consultation and feedback from stakeholders.

In 25 OECD countries,[2] a participatory process is mandatory for all primary laws, and in 20 OECD countries[3] it is mandatory for all subordinate regulations, with draft laws generally posted for four weeks for consultation (OECD, 2018[52]). In France, the website https://parlement-et-citoyens.fr enables citizens to participate in the drafting process of laws currently being prepared by Parliament, and in most EU countries there is a central website for consultation on draft laws by the administration. Table 7.1 shows some examples.

Table 7.1. Selected consultation portals

Country	Description of portal	Link to portal
Austria	Since September 2017, all draft primary laws have been available on the website of Parliament, together with a short description of the legislative project in accessible language, the RIA and other accompanying documents. The public can submit comments on the draft regulation or support comments made by others online.	https://www.parlament.gv.at/PAKT/MESN/
Croatia	On the interactive consultation portal e-Savjetovanja, major draft regulations are published for consultation for a minimum of 30 days. The website allows the public to provide general feedback on the draft or to provide comments on the individual articles of a draft regulation. The comments are publicly displayed alongside the draft, allowing other members of the public or policy makers to react. For major draft primary laws, RIA statements are also made available for comments.	https://savjetovanja.gov.hr/
Estonia	The Electronic Coordination System for Draft Legislation (EIS) tracks the development of all Estonian and EU draft legal acts, and makes available RIAs and documents of legislative intent (describing the problem to be addressed, analysing policy options and determining initial likely impacts). The website www.osale.ee/ is an interactive website of all ongoing consultations where every member of the public can submit comments on legislative proposals or other policy documents prepared by the government and review comments made by others. EIS and www.osale.ee/ are linked, and EIS takes into consideration opinions submitted via www.osale.ee/ and provides a direct link to them.	http://eelnoud.valitsus.ee/main#v9VrpqB6 www.osale.ee/
Greece	The Greek government publishes draft laws and explanatory material on its central consultation portal to the general public. It allows the public to comment separately on individual proposed clauses in a virtual "discussion room" where members of the public and policy makers can react and add further comments. Comments received during the consultation period are presented to the Greek Parliament, along with the draft law and other relevant materials.	www.opengov.gr/home/category/consultations
Netherlands	Major draft regulations are published on the Dutch central consultation portal www.internetconsultatie.nl/, and the public can visibly publish comments on the drafts as well as a summary of the impact assessment. The use of the website has been further promoted in recent years and is more frequently used to consult on policy documents that inform about the nature of the problem and possible solutions.	www.internetconsultatie.nl/

Source: OECD (2019[53]), *Better Regulation Practices across the European Union*, https://doi.org/10.1787/9789264311732-en.

In OECD countries, consultations on draft laws do not occur solely on an online portal but are combined with other forms such as informal consultations, advisory groups, formal consultations with social partners and physical public meetings (OECD, 2018[52]). Economic and social councils play a vital role in the consultation with social partners. In this sense, it is timely that Lebanon aims to reinforce the role of its council in consultation with social and economic actors, and has appointed new members (Division for Sustainable Development Goals, 2018[17]).

Citizen feedback and complaint mechanisms

Enabling citizens and businesses to submit complaints about the public administration is another way of involving stakeholders in improving policies and services, as well as being a means to interact with them directly and solve individual grievances, which can lead to improving trust in the public administration. In Lebanon there is currently no ombudsman office, despite the adoption of Law No. 664 of 2015, which is still awaiting implementation (implementation of this law is included in the National Anti-corruption Strategy). The Central Inspection Board (CIB) receives complaints from citizens, and its function is to monitor the actions of the public administration and propose improvements. Any citizen can "lodge a complaint against any public administrative department that is submitted to the authority of the Central Inspection or against the employees and workers of that department".[4] Complaints can be submitted in person in the office in Beirut, which also allows for the submission of anonymous complaints via the website of the CIB or its mobile application. The CIB, through the information and data it collects on the functioning or malfunctioning of the public administration, therefore plays a vital role for open government reforms as it can advise the public administration on reforms to undertake. In order to enable citizens and other stakeholders, such as the media and civil society, to play their role as watchdog and promote reforms, the CIB could also consider publishing data about its investigations, such as aggregated data about complaints, that highlight the themes and institutions concerned. In order to further facilitate the submission and follow-up of complaints and improve the quality of public services, the CIB could also facilitate direct contact between citizens and their administrations. For instance, in Morocco the national portal "chikaya.ma" (launched in January 2018) enables citizens to file complaints identifying the organisation concerned and to contact the administration and make suggestions for improving public service provision. Citizens can also express their level of satisfaction after their issue is addressed. The administration commits to addressing complaints within defined deadlines.

OMSAR has taken first steps towards engaging stakeholders in improving the quality of public services and in enabling them to provide feedback. The OECD survey found that OMSAR conducted two polls in 2019 on its website, one regarding the importance of interacting with public and private sectors using a digital ID and one regarding the prioritisation of digital services. This is an important step to involving stakeholders in policy and service design. However, the ability to strengthen citizen confidence depends on the feedback loop. Therefore, it would be advisable for OMSAR to provide information about the outcome of the polls and how they have been used to transform/inform policy making.

Recommendations:

- **Consider the establishment of an open government stakeholder network, bringing together different levels and branches of government with civil society organisations involved in the promotion of different elements of Lebanon's open government agenda, including the thematic group on peace of the SDG committee.**
- **Adopt an inclusive and collaborative process in the design and roll-out of the e-participation platform for the consultation process of draft laws by involving diverse stakeholders.** Lebanon could consider including a dedicated section in the planned e-participation platform for the consultation process of draft laws. Importantly, the government should equally consider combining these efforts with offline participation opportunities.
- **Strengthen stakeholder feedback and complaints mechanisms by further developing the interface between the administration and citizens.** Such an initiative should allow direct contact with relevant institutions, facilitate complaint processing and case-by-case communication, and provide systematic feedback. The interface should also be able to provide an overview of the indicators and figures related to the complaints received and addressed.

Notes

1 https://www.oecd.org/gov/open-government-toolkit-navigator.htm.

2 For other four countries it is mandatory for some primary laws and for another four countries for major primary laws. The data cover 34 OECD countries and the European Union.

3 For other eight countries it is mandatory for major subordinate regulations and for another four countries for some subordinate regulations.

4 http://www.cib.gov.lb/website.htm.

References

Division for Sustainable Development Goals (2018), *Lebanon: Voluntary National Review on Sustainable Development Goals*, United Nations, https://sustainabledevelopment.un.org/content/documents/19484Lebanon_VNR_2018.pdf (accessed on 29 October 2019). [6]

Government of Lebanon (2019), *Lebanon Digital Transformation: Strategies to Actions*. [9]

Lebanese Oil and Gas Initiative (2017), *Environmental Impact of Petroleum Activities in Lebanon*, https://logi-lebanon.org/uploaded/2017/10/5ODZQNGL_SEA%20Report%20final.pdf (accessed on 29 October 2019). [7]

Lebanese Petroleum Administration (2019), *Strategic Environmental Assessment 2019*, https://www.lpa.gov.lb/SEA_2019.php (accessed on 29 October 2019). [8]

OECD (2019), *Better Regulation Practices across the European Union*, OECD Publishing, Paris, https://doi.org/10.1787/9789264311732-en (accessed on 29 October 2019). [11]

OECD (2018), *OECD Regulatory Policy Outlook 2018*, OECD Publishing, Paris, https://dx.doi.org/10.1787/9789264303072-en. [10]

OECD (2017), *Recommendation of the Council on Open Government*, https://legalinstruments.oecd.org/en/instruments/OECD-LEGAL-0438. [1]

OECD (2016), *Open Government: The Global Context and the Way Forward*, OECD Publishing, Paris, https://dx.doi.org/10.1787/9789264268104-en. [2]

OECD (2012), *Regulatory Consultation: A MENA-OECD practitioners' guide for engaging stakeholders in the rule-making process*, OECD, Paris, https://www.oecd.org/mena/governance/MENA-Practitioners-Guide-%20EN.pdf (accessed on 29 October 2019). [3]

OECD (2001), *Citizens as Partners: OECD Handbook on Information, Consultation and Public Participation in Policy-Making*, OECD Publishing, https://doi.org/10.1787/9789264195578-en (accessed on 15 November 2019). [4]

Participedia (2020), *"Methods" webpage*, https://participedia.net/?selectedCategory=method (accessed on 2 July 2020). [5]

Chapter 8. Open state

Open government is a culture of governance that does not only apply to the executive branch of the state, but that can apply to all state institutions. Despite most open government initiatives worldwide focusing on the executive, countries are designing specific strategies and initiatives for an “open judiciary”, “open parliament”, “open subnational government” and “open independent institutions”, or are even adopting an open state approach. Costa Rica for example signed the first-ever Declaration for the Creation of an Open State in 2016, and Colombia is the first country to elaborate an Open State Policy (OECD, 2019[6]). An open state is “when all public institutions of the executive, parliament and the judiciary, independent public institutions, and all levels of government join forces and collaborate with civil society, academia, the media and the private sector to design and implement a reform agenda to make public governance more transparent, accountable and participatory” (OECD, 2016[2]).The OECD therefore recommends that states “promote a progressive move from the concept of open government towards that of open state, while recognising the respective roles, prerogatives and overall independence of all concerned parties” (OECD, 2016[2]).

In Lebanon, the prime minister and the minister of state for administrative reform are currently leading the country's open government reform efforts. Open government initiatives can also be found at the subnational level. As Chapter 10 shows, the municipalities of Shweir and Byblos have been adopting some initiatives to promote the principles of transparency, stakeholder participation, integrity and accountability.

Open Parliament:

Lebanon's Parliament also plays a crucial role in open government efforts: it is where key legislation related to open government principles is adopted, and it can be a means to engage stakeholders in policy making and legislative deliberations. Greater openness of Parliament would enable stakeholders to participate in the law-making process and in holding government to account (OECD, 2016[2]). The Declaration on Parliamentary Openness (see Box 8.1) provides a set of principles that can guide parliaments in strengthening openness.

Box 8.1. Declaration on Parliamentary Openness

This declaration was elaborated through an inclusive and open process and is a call by civil society parliamentary monitoring organisations for greater openness. It was adopted in 2012 and includes principles that legislative bodies can follow to strengthen their openness. These principles are listed below:

Promoting a culture of openness

1. Recognising public ownership of parliamentary information
2. Advancing a culture of openness through legislation
3. Protecting a culture of openness through oversight
4. Promoting civic education
5. Engaging citizens and civil society
6. Protecting an independent civil society
7. Enabling effective parliamentary monitoring
8. Sharing good practice
9. Ensuring legal recourse
10. Disseminating complete information
11. Providing timely information
12. Ensuring accurate information

Making parliamentary information transparent

13. Adopting policies on parliamentary transparency
14. Providing information on parliament's roles and functions
15. Providing information on members of parliament
16. Providing information on parliamentary staff and administration
17. Informing citizens regarding the parliamentary agenda
18. Engaging citizens on draft legislation
19. Publishing records of committee proceedings
20. Recording parliamentary votes
21. Publishing records of plenary proceedings
22. Publishing reports created by or provided to parliament
23. Providing information on the budget and expenditure
24. Disclosing assets and ensuring the integrity of members
25. Disclosing information on unethical conduct and potential conflicts of interest
26. Providing access to historical information

Easing access to parliamentary information

27. Providing multiple channels for accessing information
28. Ensuring physical access
29. Guaranteeing access by the media
30. Providing live and on-demand broadcasts and streaming

31. Facilitating access throughout the country
32. Using plain language
33. Using multiple national or working languages
34. Granting free access

Enabling electronic communication of parliamentary information

35. Providing information in open and structured formats
36. Ensuring technological usability
37. Protecting citizen privacy
38. Using non-proprietary formats and open-source software
39. Allowing downloadability for reuse
40. Maintaining parliamentary websites
41. Using easy and stable search mechanisms
42. Linking related information
43. Enabling use of alert services
44. Facilitating two-way communication

Source: OpeningParliament.org (2012[54]), *Declaration on Parliamentary Openness*, www.openingparliament.org/declaration.

Lebanon has a unicameral system with a National Assembly that is elected for a term of four years by universal suffrage. The last parliamentary elections were held in 2018, following several years of extended mandates as political tumults and legislative changes were preventing the timely organisation of elections. According to the 1989 Ṭaif Accord, which ended the civil war in Lebanon, parliamentary seats are apportioned equally between Christian and Muslim sects. As all large political factions in the country and in Parliament are also part of the government there is no opposition in Parliament, which means that its traditional accountability function is restricted. For example, according to interviews with parliamentarians, Parliament has only held one session to question the government since it was elected in 2018. The questions and interrogations by parliamentarians are published on the website of the Assembly, however the last update was in 2012.

Questioning government is a common practice in OECD countries, and a key function of parliament is to play an oversight role. The Lebanese Parliament could consider institutionalising this practice more regularly, as per Article 131[1] of the Rules of Procedure of Parliament,[2] by opening up such question sessions to stakeholders. It could proactively communicate about these sessions beforehand and invite stakeholders, such as civil society and the media, to participate and act as watchdogs. Parliament's sessions are public, unless the majority decides to hold them in private at the request of the government or at least five deputies (Article 51, unofficial translation).

Another way that Parliament's oversight function has been diminished is through the adoption of the 2019 Budget Law without discussing the latest audit report of the budget – the 2017 report. A law was passed to allow for this change in procedure and the 2017 audit report was not made public. As discussed in Chapter 6, the budget is a key tool to decide policy priorities and its transparency is therefore of paramount importance. Parliament could consider discussing the draft budget law and the audit report in public sessions and making all relevant documents accessible to the public.

According to the findings of the Gherbal Initiative (2019[11]), Parliament could enhance its application of the Right of Access to Information Law by appointing an official responsible for access to information and providing training and awareness raising about the law and its implications to staff and elected members. These open state efforts could mirror those currently underway to include active judicial disclosures (e.g.

court rulings, consultative and judicial decisions and annual reports) as part of the implementation of the Right of Access to Information Law and related e-portal.

Parliament is taking the first steps to provide access to relevant information. All laws adopted by Parliament are published on its website.[3] This is of particular importance, as accessing the law as published in the official gazette is not free. The laws are however only searchable by year and session, not by title or topic of law. Parliament could consider making this section of its website more user-friendly. The website includes other features to provide information, such as members of the parliamentary committees which are published in a single pdf document.[4] The minutes of sessions were last updated in 2013. The website also includes some information on upcoming meetings of Parliament. This website could become a hub for information regarding Parliament's work through a more user-friendly design and more up-to-date information regarding, for example, minutes and draft laws under discussion.

Publishing draft laws for public information and even for public consultation is a common practice in OECD countries. As discussed in Chapter 7, Circular No. 21/2012 requires all public entities to publish draft legal texts on government websites and solicit consultation and feedback from stakeholders. Given this legal backing, Parliament could consider publishing draft laws before they are discussed in Parliament sessions, and inviting stakeholders to these discussions, which is of even greater importance as participation in committee meetings is invitation only.

There are ongoing efforts led by the Parliamentarians against Corruption, in partnership with the Westminster Foundation to enhance Parliament's openness. These efforts include the drafting of a strategic plan for Parliament, which has not yet been approved, as well as suggestions to amend some of the Rules of Procedure to allow for greater openness, participation and digitalisation of the Assembly. As such, Parliament could build on the current momentum and the country's commitment to open government to advance its own open government initiatives. It could create an informal working group of parliamentarians and administrative staff committed to open government principles to elaborate an action plan of initiatives to undertake, to disseminate the concept in Parliament and to co-ordinate efforts with the national government. The French and Moroccan parliaments, for example, adopted their own national action plans on parliamentary openness, which could serve as inspiration (see Box 8.2).

Box 8.2. Parliamentary open government action plans

French National Assembly

France adopted the National Action Plan on Parliamentary Openness within the framework of the Open Government Partnership (OGP) programme in July 2015. The French National Assembly committed itself to strengthening the transparency of the legislative process and increasing the involvement of citizens in the work of the National Assembly. The National Assembly voluntarily engaged with the government in this process. Furthermore, in July 2017 the Presidency of the National Assembly launched "*Rendez-vous des réformes 2017-2022*", a process designed to "modernise the Assembly by making it more transparent, more efficient and more open in its operation". The resulting second Parliamentary Action Plan includes 17 commitments clustered under four axes:

1. **The comprehensive approach to reforming the national assembly**: "For a New National Assembly: The 2017-2022 Reform Meetings" aims to comprehensively modernise the functioning of the National Assembly through the application of an open, participatory and transparent methodology.
2. **Transparency and openness**: Reporting on the functioning of the National Assembly is a fundamental principle that builds trust between citizens and their elected representatives. Commitments essential to the re-establishment of strong links between the institution and civil society are presented, including the open-source publication of the National Assembly's source codes or the publication of new datasets on the open data platform.
3. **Citizen participation**: This section presents four commitments that aim to enable citizens to participate more actively in the functioning of the National Assembly, whether at work or using the data it produces and disseminates (open data) via the development of citizen consultations, for example.
4. **Better publicising parliamentary work**: Different institutional actors are responsible for bringing parliamentary work to the attention of citizens. Members of Parliament and the National Assembly must also exploit the possibilities offered by digital technology to communicate their actions by offering training in the use of new technologies or by diversifying the institution's digital communications.

National action plan of Morocco's House of Representatives (2019-2020)

In line with the Constitutional principles, Morocco's House of Representatives initiated a reform process to modernise its working methods and ensure greater openness and communication with citizens. Parliament decided to participate in Morocco's OGP process and included several commitments in the OGP Action Plan. These include:

- Implementing the constitutional and legislative provisions on citizen and participatory democracy.
- Involvement of citizens in the legislative process.
- Implementing the access to information provisions.
- Opening up to the public, with a focus on youth.

- Citizen consultation and engagement in policy evaluation.
- Creating a partnership with civil society and academia.

Source: Government of France (2018), "Gouvernement et Parlement ouverts: la France renouvelle son engagement pour une action publique transparente et collaborative" [Open Government and Parliament: France Renews its Commitment to Transparent and Collaborative Public Action] (accessed 30 June 2020).

Recommendations:

- **Parliament could consider institutionalising the practice of questioning government more regularly and allowing question sessions for stakeholder participants, such as civil society and the media.**
- **Parliament could consider discussing the draft budget law and the audit report in public sessions and making all relevant documents accessible to the public.**
- **Parliament could update its website, including with a more user-friendly design and more current information regarding minutes and draft laws under discussion.**
- **Parliament could consider publishing draft laws before they are discussed in Parliamentary sessions and inviting stakeholders to these discussions.**
- **Parliament could create an informal working group of parliamentarians and administrative staff committed to open government principles**. This group could elaborate an action plan of initiatives to undertake, disseminate the concept in Parliament and co-ordinate efforts with the national government.
- **Parliament could enhance its application of the Right of Access to Information Law by appointing an official responsible for access to information.** The duties of this role could also include providing training and awareness raising about the law and its implications to staff and elected members.

Notes

[1] "Any one or more deputies may request the questioning of the government as a whole or a minister in a particular matter" (Article 131, unofficial translation).

[2] Rules of procedure published in the official gazette No. 52 on 13/11/2003 www.lp.gov.lb/CustomPage.aspx?id=37&masterId=1.

[3] www.lp.gov.lb/ViewLawYears.aspx.

[4] www.lp.gov.lb/Resources/Files/fea96655-3ae4-43b0-accd-f4bd6c560299.pdf.

References

Gherbal Initiative (2019), *Transparency in Lebanese Public Administrations*, http://elgherbal.org/projects/view/en/8 (accessed on 29 October 2019). [4]

OECD (2019), *Open Government in Argentina*, OECD Public Governance Reviews, OECD Publishing, Paris, https://dx.doi.org/10.1787/1988ccef-en. [1]

OECD (2016), *Open Government: The Global Context and the Way Forward*, OECD Publishing, Paris, https://dx.doi.org/10.1787/9789264268104-en. [2]

OpeningParliament.org (2012), *Declaration on Parliamentary Openness*, http://www.openingparliament.org/declaration (accessed on 29 October 2019). [3]

Chapter 9. Lebanon's performance against Open Government Partnership minimum eligibility criteria

To join the Open Government Partnership (OGP), governments commit to upholding the principles of open and transparent government by endorsing the Open Government Declaration. Members must also meet the eligibility criteria and pass the OGP values check. Prior to submitting the first action plan, OGP members should identify responsible government departments and engage with civil society for a clear and open process of participation.[1] Aspiring OGP members need to obtain 12 out of 16 possible points, according to the OGP minimum eligibility criteria,[2] in order to join the OGP. Lebanon currently has 8 points, as noted in Table 9.1.

Table 9.1. OGP minimum eligibility requirements: Lebanon's current status

Criteria	Lebanon's current status	Lebanon's score
Budget transparency • 2 points if the executive budget proposal is published. • 2 points if the audit report is published.	The executive budget proposal and audit report have not been published for most recent years.	0/4
Access to information • 4 points for access to information laws in place. • 3 points for a constitutional provision guaranteeing access to information. • 1 point for draft access to information law under consideration.	Right of Access to Information Law No. 28 adopted in 2017.	4/4
Disclosures related to elected or senior public officials • 4 points for a law requiring officials to submit asset disclosures that are accessible to the public. • 2 points for a law requiring officials to submit asset disclosures.	Legislation mandates that declarations are required by law but are yet not made public.	2/4
Citizen participation (based on civil liberty indicator of EIU Democracy Index) • 4 points for countries scoring above 7.5 • 3 points for countries scoring above 5 • 2 points for countries scoring above 2.5	Score of 4.71/10 in the civil liberty indicator of the EIU Democracy Index 2019.	2/4
Total	(12 points needed to become eligible to join the OGP)	8/16

As noted above, Lebanon approved the Law on the Right of Access to Information in January 2017, which affords a score of 4/4 points. Regarding budget transparency, two points are awarded for the publication of two essential documents for open budgets: the executive budget proposal and audit report. This criteria uses a subset indicator from the Open Budget Index, conducted by the International Budget Partnership, which covers 100 countries. Latest research shows that Lebanon has 0 points as it has not published the most recent versions of the executive budget proposal and the audit report.

Regarding disclosures related to elected or senior public officials, an updated Law on Asset and Interest Declaration and the Fight against Illicit Enrichment was adopted on 30 September 2020, which further specifics the scope and obligations related to asset disclosures of public officials; however as of writing, , the declarations are not published or made public. Lebanon therefore scores 2 out of 4 in this category and should consider the public disclosure of assets and a system to verify the accuracy of declarations to enhance its effectiveness.

Lebanon's score regarding citizen participation is due to the country's position in the sub indicator on civil liberties of the Economist Intelligent Unit's (EIU) Democracy Index. Lebanon scored 4.71/10 in this Civil Liberty indicator of the EIU Democracy Index 2019 which leads to an OGP score of 2/4 points.

OGP values check assessment

Following a decision of the OGP's steering committee on 20 September 2017, countries must also pass a values check assessment, in addition to the abovementioned eligibility criteria, before they are allowed to participate in the OGP. To pass the values check, countries must score three or higher in at least one of the following V-Dem indicators:

- **Civil society organisation (CSO) entry and exit**: Measures the extent to which the government achieves control over entry and exit by CSOs into public life.
- **CSO repression**: Measures the extent to which the government attempts to repress CSOs.

Lebanon currently scores 3 for CSO entry and exit and 3 for CSO repression according to the 2019 V-Dem survey, and as a result, passes the OGP value check.

Recommendations:

- **To improve the budget transparency score, consider publishing executive budget proposals and audit reports for recent years, and continue publishing them on an annual basis.**
- **To improve scores related to disclosures of elected or senior public officials, consider the public disclosure of assets and a system to verify the accuracy of the declarations.**
- **To improve the citizen participation score, additional focus could be placed on the implementation of ongoing open government reforms to improve the results of indices measuring civil liberties, CSO entry and exit, and CSO repression.**

Notes

[1] www.opengovpartnership.org/.

[2] www.opengovpartnership.org/eligibility.

Chapter 10. Open government scan of selected Lebanese municipalities

Introduction

The current context of Lebanon expressing an interest to adhere to the 2017 OECD Recommendation of the Council on Open Government (hereafter "the Recommendation") and to join the Open Government Partnership (OGP) offers an opportunity to foster a new culture of open governance at the municipal as well as national level. Taking into account the commitment of the national government to promote open government principles and initiatives, two municipalities that have engaged in transparency, integrity, accountability and stakeholder participation efforts were selected to participate in a scan and capacity building exercise with the OECD. These municipalities are Byblos (known locally as "Jbeil") and Shweir – Ain Sindyneh (referred to as "Shweir" hereafter). The objective of this scan is to review the institutional policy frameworks and open government practices and initiatives in the municipality in order to align them with OECD standards, increase their impact, and disseminate their best practices and lessons learned with other Lebanese municipalities. Open local authorities are also an important part of a country's transition from open government to open state.

The following open government scan was developed on the basis of the OECD survey of open government in Byblos and Shweir, as well as interviews with the mayors, councillors, municipal administration and local civil society in September 2019 and February 2019.

The OECD's framework for open government at the local level

The OECD defines open government as "a culture of governance that promotes the principles of transparency, integrity, accountability and stakeholder participation in support of democracy and inclusive growth" (OECD, 2017[1]). These four principles are enshrined in the Recommendation and can be defined as follows:

- **Transparency** refers to "the disclosure and subsequent accessibility of relevant government data and information" (OECD, 2016[2]).
- **Integrity** is the "consistent alignment of, and adherence to, shared ethical values, principles and norms for upholding and prioritising the public interests in the public sector" (OECD, 2017[55]).
- **Accountability** refers to the "government's responsibility and duty to inform its citizens about the decisions it makes, as well as to provide an account of the activities and performance of the entire government and its officials" (OECD, 2016[2]).
- **Stakeholder participation** refers to " all the ways in which stakeholders can be involved in the policy cycle and in service design and delivery, including:
    - **Information:** An initial level of participation characterised by a one-way relationship in which the government produces and delivers information to stakeholders. It covers both on-demand provision of information and "proactive" measures by the government to disseminate information.

- **Consultation:** A more advanced level of participation that entails a two-way relationship in which stakeholders provide feedback to the government and vice versa. It is based on the prior definition of the issue for which views are being sought and requires the provision of relevant information, in addition to feedback on the outcomes of the process.
- **Engagement:** When stakeholders are given the opportunity and the necessary resources (e.g. information, data and digital tools) to collaborate during all phases of the policy cycle and in the service design and delivery" (OECD, 2017[1]).

Local administrations are central to initiatives for more transparent, accountable and participatory governance. They are an essential interface for citizens to be in contact with public policies and services, which has resulted in many of the most innovative approaches to open government coming from cities, regions or provinces. As they are responsible for delivering public services, such as road maintenance, sanitation and policing, local governments form the most immediate relationships between public administrations and citizens. This was outlined in the OECD report "Open Government: The Global Context and the Way Forward":

> *The proximity of citizens and the state spurs engagement, but also shapes citizens' perception about the government. Thus, it is not surprising that cities, regions or provinces have, in the last decades, been places for citizen engagement. The demands for greater engagement of citizens in urban planning date back to the 60/70s. Innovative and interactive approaches to involve citizens in policy making arose in parallel with the decentralisation efforts by many countries from the 1970s and consisted of transferring authority, responsibility and resources from the national government to lower governmental levels, to better respond to citizens' needs and demands" (OECD, 2016[2]).*

To achieve successful reforms, local authorities must first adopt a new culture of governance that promotes the four open government principles. This requires strong political will and enabling institutions and a consistent whole-of-government approach, as well as the necessary human, financial and technical resources and a forward-looking attitude to promote innovation and apply digital tools.

This chapter will assess open government policies and initiatives in Shweir and Byblos across the three pillars of the OECD's Recommendation on Open Government: the enabling environment, implementation and the way ahead (Figure 10.1). The first pillar regards the strategic, legal and regulatory frameworks; human, financial and technical resources; and open government literacy. The second pillar focuses on the implementation frameworks necessary to carry out open government initiatives and practices, including the co-ordination mechanisms across government, monitoring and evaluation, communication, access to information, and stakeholder participation processes. The third pillar concerns the most forward-looking aspects of the open government agenda, public sector innovation, and includes digital tools and open government data and the idea of moving towards an "open state" where all public institutions – not just government – have an open government culture and practices in place.

Figure 10.1. Three pillars: 10 provisions for the governance of open government

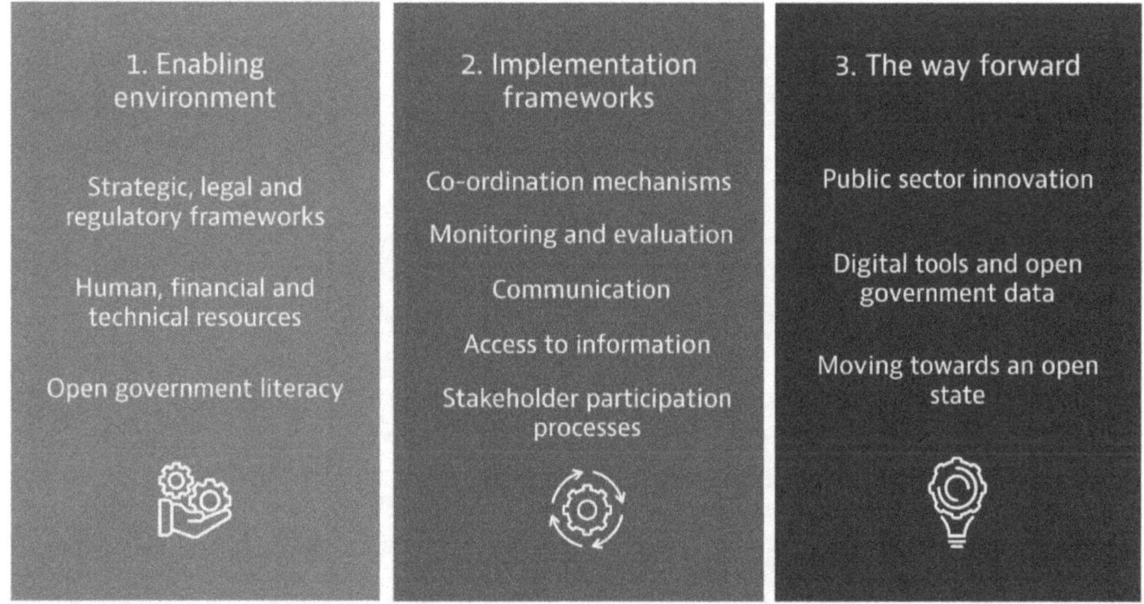

Source: OECD (2017[11]), *Recommendation of the Council on Open Government*, https://legalinstruments.oecd.org/en/instruments/OECD-LEGAL-0438.

The following sections provide the context regarding the mandate of municipalities in Lebanon, the state of play of decentralisation reforms and an overview of open government principles at a local level.

Municipal powers in Lebanon

Lebanon is a unitary state and its public administration is organised into three levels: central administration, deconcentrated administration (8 governorates and 26 districts) and decentralised administration (1 138 municipalities and 57 municipal unions) (Figure 10.2).

Figure 10.2. Higher and lower government tiers in Lebanon

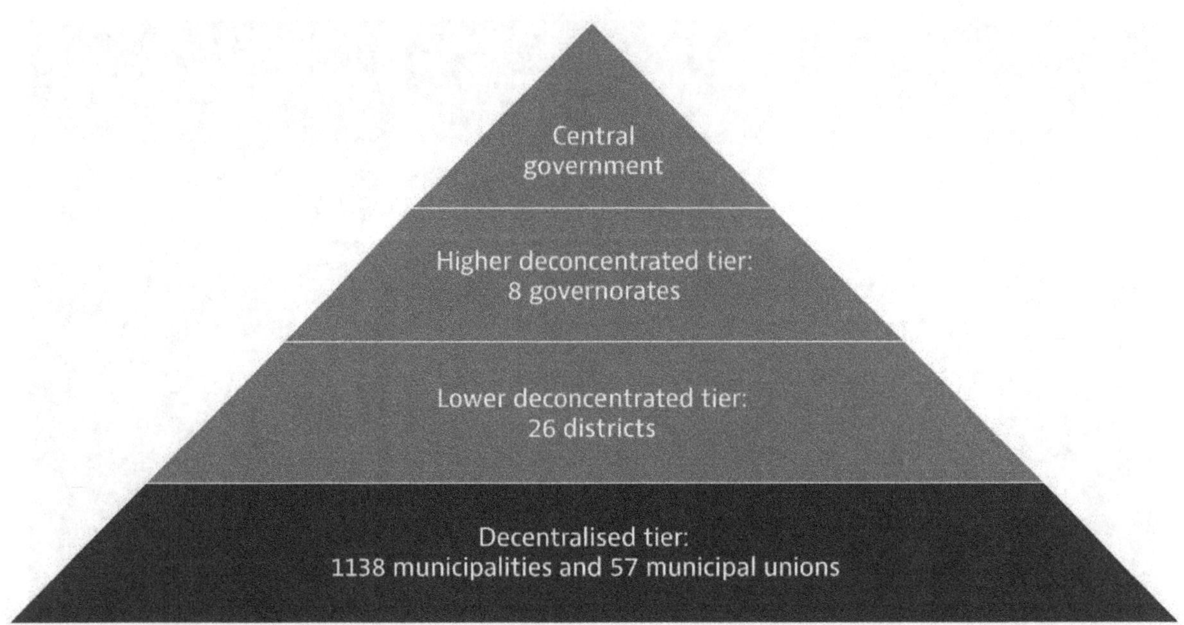

Source: Democracy Reporting International (2017[56]), *Reforming Decentralisation in Lebanon: The State of Play*, https://democracy-reporting.org/dri_publications/bp-80-reforming-decentralisation-in-lebanon-the-state-of-play/.

Central administration

The central administration refers to the president, prime minister, Council of Ministers and ministers, as well as ministries and central councils with administrative powers. Executive authority is centralised and the central public administration plays a key role in Lebanon's governance.

Deconcentrated administration

In many countries where power is centralised, there is a deconcentrated system to lessen the central government's administrative burden and to bring decision making closer to citizens in economic, social, education and /or health affairs. In Lebanon, territories are divided into geographical units called governorates, and the state's administrative authority is extended to central administration representatives who have decision-making authority regarding local affairs. There are eight governorates in Lebanon: Akkar: Baalbek-Hermel, Beirut, Beqaa, Mount Lebanon, Nabatiyeh, North Lebanon and South Lebanon.

Governorates are divided into 26 districts (called *qadas*), with the exception of the Beirut governorate, which is not sub-divided. These are smaller geographical units where decision-making power on behalf of central government is granted to district commissioners.

The governorates and districts form the upper and lower deconcentrated tiers of the central government respectively. They are therefore not legal entities as they represent the central government, constituting an integral part of the Ministry of Interior and Municipality (MOIM), which is responsible for policies related to the governorates, districts, municipalities, municipal unions[1] and villages (Democracy Reporting International, 2017[56]; The Lebanese Center for Policy Studies, 2015[57]).

Administrative decentralisation

Lebanon has one decentralised tier of administration, which is comprised of 1 138 municipalities and 57 municipal unions. Three-quarters (75%) of municipalities are part of a municipal union (Democracy Reporting International, 2017[56]). These local units are defined by geographical areas and are governed by elected councils, which have legal powers related to citizens' affairs at the local level. Lebanese citizens are registered to vote in the location of their family's origin, meaning that many people do not vote where they reside. This underlines the need to have strong stakeholder participation policies in place at the municipal level to bring citizens closer to government and provide them with an opportunity to influence local public decisions.

The elected council holds the policy-making power, while the mayor (elected by the councillors) holds a chief executive role and chairs the executive authority.[2] Article 47 of the Municipal Act (1977) sets out a broad range of duties for municipalities: "Each work of public character or interest in the municipal area falls within the scope of the municipal council's competence." However, conflicting legislative texts, administrative and fiscal blockages, and heavy central government control limit municipalities' autonomy (Democracy Reporting International, 2017[56]; Democracy Reporting International, 2019[58]). As in some OECD countries, municipalities are responsible for providing local services such as street cleaning; road tarmacking; public lighting; street signs; urban planning; selected aspects of healthcare, education, and social affairs; sometimes public order; and wastewater management and water drainage (OECD/UCLG, 2016[59]).

Municipality funding comes from the Independent Municipal Fund (IMF) and from local taxes. The IMF is an intergovernmental grant system that transfers taxes and fees from central to local governments. The central government distributes the funds based on a formula outlined in Decree 1917 of 1979. Article 87 of the Municipal Act states that "the revenues and common allowances of all municipalities shall be deposited in trust in an independent municipal fund at the Ministry of Interior". The amount allocated to each municipality is calculated as follows: 60% based on the registered population and 40% based on direct revenues collected in the previous two years (Atallah, 2011[60]). On average, 36% of municipalities' revenue comes from the IMF and the rest is raised through local taxes (Mourad and Piron, 2016[61]).

The state of play for decentralisation in Lebanon

The groundwork for decentralisation was laid in the Ta'if Agreement[3] in 1989, which set out "extensive administrative decentralisation" to foster "even development" between different Lebanese regions (Democracy Reporting International, 2017[56]). The agreement was integrated into the Constitution in 1990, mandating a comprehensive decentralisation reform. There have been numerous attempts to adopt a new legal framework for decentralisation since 1991, none of which have yet been adopted. The most recent of these was the draft Administrative Decentralisation Bill in 2014, championed by the former Minister of the Interior and Municipalities, Ziyad Baroud (Box 10.1).

Box 10.1. The 2014 Administrative Decentralisation Bill

The 2014 Administrative Decentralisation bill included the following provisions:

1. "Division of Lebanon into 33 regions with regional councils that are granted a wide scope of work, and suppression of the lower deconcentrated tier (districts).
2. Elections on the basis of proportional representation instead of the so far adopted first-past-the-post system.
3. Improved transparency and mandatory use of ICT and e-government.
4. Institutionalised participation mechanisms and civic oversight at the local level.
5. Promotion of public-private partnerships in local governance.
6. Adoption of a gender quota in the electoral law.
7. A sustainable fiscal and financial system."

Source: Democracy Reporting International (2017[56]), *Reforming Decentralisation in Lebanon: The State of Play*, https://democracy-reporting.org/dri_publications/bp-80-reforming-decentralisation-in-lebanon-the-state-of-play/.

As outlined above, the draft bill includes numerous propositions that enhance the open government principles of transparency, integrity, accountability and stakeholder participation. It introduces innovations that Lebanese civil society has been advocating for many years related to digital government, increased transparency, institutionalised civic participation and scrutiny, electoral reform, as well as greater administrative and financial autonomy. However, it does not mention municipalities or their legal framework, nor does it mention reform of the municipal electoral system regarding the ability of residents to vote. At the time of writing, the draft Administrative Decentralisation Bill has not been adopted.

Open government principles at the municipal level

The open government principles of transparency, integrity, accountability and participation are enshrined, although not always explicitly, in the Municipal Act of 1977. Article 45 states the right of voters or interested parties to obtain copies of the municipal decisions that may be disclosed to the public. Article 55 stipulates that council decisions that are in force and serve a public interest must be posted on the door of the municipal premises. Furthermore, Article 76 states that decisions of public character issued by the head of the executive authority (the mayor) must be posted on the municipal council's door. However, the Municipal Act also includes clauses that go against the open government principles, notably Article 35 which states that municipal council sessions are held in secrecy.

More recently, the Right of Access to Information Law (2017) requires central institutions and municipalities to publish all public administrative documents (decisions, budgets, annual accounts and tenders), create special websites for this purpose, and reply to access to information (ATI) requests. More details about the implementation status of this law are available in Chapter 3.

The legal and regulatory frameworks for local governance in Lebanon do not require local authorities to engage with and consult citizens in decision making, public policy making and planning. However, Democracy Reporting International's (DRI) recent survey in Lebanon shows that half of municipal unions do engage in participation (Democracy Reporting International, 2019[58]), although information about participation at the level of municipalities is missing. DRI and the Lebanese Transparency Association are carrying out numerous pilot projects and capacity building activities on participation in municipalities across Lebanon.

The principles of open government could be strengthened at the municipal level through legal amendments to the Municipal Act and the draft Administrative Decentralisation Bill by requiring councils to open their sessions, declassify their session reports, and making it binding to publish council decisions. Moreover, introducing amendments to establish mandatory stakeholder participation could ensure that citizens are consulted and engaged regularly in planning, infrastructure and other local public policy decisions.

Overall context

Municipality of Byblos

Byblos is the largest city in the Mount Lebanon governorate and is situated around 40 km to the north of Beirut along the coast. It is a UNESCO World Heritage Site for its structures that are testimony to the beginnings of the Phoenician civilisation and is known as being one of the oldest continually inhabited cities in the world, with evidence of communities occupying the site for at least 8 000 years.

The municipality's inhabitants are predominantly Christian, mostly Maronite, with a minority of Shia Muslims. There are no data available about the population age breakdown. Byblos is home to professional schools of the Lebanese American University, and its economy relies heavily on tourism due to its ancient port, Phoenician, Roman, and Crusader ruins, beaches, and surrounding mountains. Given its proximity to Beirut, some inhabitants commute to work in the capital.

Municipality of Shweir and Ain Sindyaneh

Shweir is a municipality in the Matn region of Mount Lebanon, 30 km from Beirut. It comprises the towns of Dhour Shweir and Ain Sindyaneh. According to interviews with the municipality, as of May 2019 it has a population of 6 000 in the peak summer season, and a population of around 4 500 the rest of the year. The vast majority of Shweir's population are of working age (between 20 and 65 Table 10.1), and there are a significant number of immigrants (estimated at around 30% of the overall population, although as there are no precise figures the overall population estimate excludes immigrants), mostly from Syria.

Table 10.1. Population of Shweir by age

Age	Number of residents
Under 20	700
20-40	2 000
40-65	2 000
65+	300

Note: These figures exclude refugees and emigrants.
Source: Estimates by Shweir municipality, May 2019.

The economy revolves around summer tourism, commerce and banking. Many people work in and commute to Beirut daily. Shweir is not part of a municipality union; however, there is informal exchange between the mayors of Shweir and neighbouring municipalities about common issues, such as security and local events.

The enabling environment

Developing an open government strategy and institutionalising good practices

In order to create a framework for all open government reforms and to align related efforts in a municipality, the OECD recommends the development of an open government strategy. According to a definition in the Recommendation, "an open government strategy (is) a document that defines the open government agenda … [and] includes key open government initiatives, together with short, medium and long-term goals and indicators" (OECD, 2017[1]). Such a strategy can help to ensure that open government initiatives reinforce each other and are implemented in a way that contributes to a shared vision and common objectives. It should include high-level political commitments, as well as specific, delivery oriented commitments.

If co-created with stakeholders, an open government strategy has the potential to impact on all of local government's functions and activities, and improve the relationship between government and society. OECD data show that despite many notable open government practices at national and subnational levels in OECD countries, a consistent approach to designing and implementing open government policies and initiatives through an official strategy is often lacking.

There are numerous open government initiatives underway in Byblos and Shweir that could be included in such a strategy. These are discussed in greater detail over the course of this chapter and are summarised in Box 10.2 below.

Box 10.2. Summary of open government initiatives in Byblos and Shweir

Byblos

- Proactive disclosure of information regarding the budget.
- Regular open-door sessions with the mayor.
- Mechanism for citizens to submit complaints/suggestions through the municipality's app and social media.
- Active public communication about council activities, initiatives and municipal plans through Facebook.
- Participative processes used for developing municipal plans and urban planning.
- Citizen participation in planning different events in the city.
- Up-to-date municipality website with information about the municipality, news, projects, press coverage, a gallery and contact details.
- Data archive in development.
- Baladiyati mobile app where citizens can access information about municipality news and public services and submit complaints.
- Training and workshops conducted with civil society organisations on open government.
- Transparent procurement process.

Shweir

- Training about transparency, integrity and information technology (IT) provided for all municipal staff members.
- Proactive disclosure of information regarding the budget and council resolutions.
- Daily open door sessions with the mayor and councillors.
- Mechanism for citizens to submit complaints/suggestions through the municipality's app and social media.
- Transparent procurement process.
- Participative processes used for developing municipal plans and urban planning.
- Citizen participation in development of annual Emigrants Festival.
- Active public communication about council activities and initiatives through social media – Facebook, Instagram and Twitter.
- Tracking of audience engagement on social media.
- Data archive in development.
- Geographical Information System (GIS) in place.
- Baladiyati mobile app where citizens can access information about municipality news and public services and submit complaints.

Source: 2019 OECD open government survey of Shweir; interviews with mayor, councillors, administrative staff and civil society.

These are important efforts and demonstrate strong political will and leadership to advance open government reforms at the municipal level. They cover all four open government principles and include many practices that could be replicated across the country. At the moment, these good practices remain disparate open government initiatives and, while they are part of the mayor's strategic vision, they are not enshrined in a strategy. They are largely dependent on the political commitment and leadership of the current mayor and council.

The municipalities of Byblos and Shweir could consider developing their own open government strategies to institutionalise their open government practices, articulate their vision, establish clear objectives, and embed the principles of open government in all areas of the municipality. This is the case in a number of OECD countries, such as the city of Edmonton in Canada (see Box 10.3). Having a strategy in place would also help to enable a long-term approach and enshrine an open government culture in Byblos and Shweir, bringing the residents and stakeholders of each municipality together around the same vision. It would also help to ensure that open government initiatives are conducted to achieve wider objectives, for instance inclusive growth, strengthened democracy or increased public trust in government.

Box 10.3. Open City Initiative, Edmonton, Canada

The Open City Initiative outlines how the city council of Edmonton will advance the city's vision and strategic objectives, as defined in "The Way Ahead" which describes the vision of the city leading up to 2040. The initiative is based on five principles (transparency, participation, collaboration, innovation and inclusion) and revolves around five key goals:

Goal One: Foundational elements: The City of Edmonton's practices are aligned to support openness, transparency and consistency.

Goal Two: Open engagement: Through innovative and inclusive public engagement approaches, the city creates opportunities for people to interact with the city and impact the design, development and delivery of public programmes, services and policies. The city supports community building and leadership for engaged citizenship through education and collaboration.

Goal Three: Open data: The city will enhance the quality and increase the quantity of information available through the Open Data Programme. Through provisioning, delivering, consuming and crowdsourcing data, the city will enhance services, stimulate economic opportunities, encourage innovation and unlock new social values.

Goal Four: Open information: Information is provided to Edmontonians to promote participation and collaboration, increase knowledge and build capacity in the community.

Goal Five: Open analytics: By leveraging the vast stores of city data and new analytic capabilities, open analytics supports informed policy development and decision making. Tools and resources are provided to citizens and city staff to empower them to work with data.

Source: City of Edmonton (2017[62]), *Open City Initiative*, www.edmonton.ca/city_government/documents/Open_City_Initiative.pdf.

As outlined in the OECD Recommendation on Open Government (OECD, 2017[1]), to reach its full potential, an open government strategy should be developed with an inclusive process that results in "buy-in" from key actors in and outside of government. It is therefore important to involve all relevant stakeholders, especially citizens and civil society organisations (CSOs). In OECD countries, the types of actors involved include: government institutions, citizens, migrant communities, organised civil society, academic institutions, media/journalists, organised professional groups, international organisations and the Open Government Partnership Support Unit (OECD, 2019[16]).

The institutional framework for open government

Successfully implementing open government practices and developing an open government strategy depend on a solid institutional framework. In OECD countries, analyses demonstrate the value of dedicated structures to co-ordinate open government initiatives to ensure their consistency, complementarity and relevance (OECD, 2016[2]).

Byblos has a formalised administrative structure, as outlined in Figure 10.3. The municipality president oversees the council and all administrative departments (secretariat, finance, administration, engineering, police, health, culture and tourism). The secretariat department oversees the press department, and the engineering department oversees various other teams, such as works, cleaning and public gardens. Responsibilities that relate to open government principles are shared between the secretariat, finance, administration and tourism departments in particular. The head of tourism manages the municipality's website and the secretariat handles social media and traditional press relations. These two teams are in regular contact with the finance and administrative departments to communicate any important news and budget information to the public. As of September 2019, no one is specifically tasked with managing access to information (ATI) requests, nor is anyone responsible for stakeholder and citizen participation.

Figure 10.3. How Byblos municipality is organised

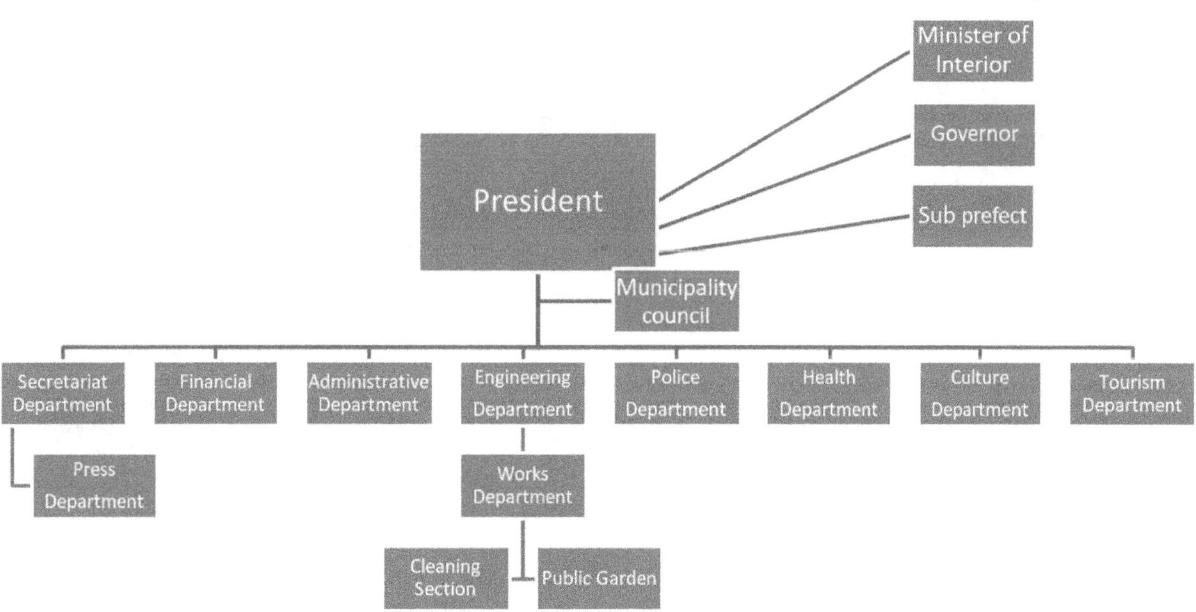

Source: Byblos municipality, September 2019.

The municipality of Shweir has a formalised administrative structure, as outlined in Figure 10.5. Scale of participatory practices: Levels of stakeholder participation. As the chief executive of the council, the mayor oversees the head of police, head of media, head of administration and head of finance. As it is a small municipality, the head of the administrative department is also charged with open government related issues, such as access to information, including answering ATI requests, and citizen participation. Horizontal co-ordination on some open government issues is well established: the head of media works with the head of administration on public communication efforts, and they also co-ordinate with the finance department regarding publicising budgetary information.

Figure 10.4. How Shweir municipality is organised

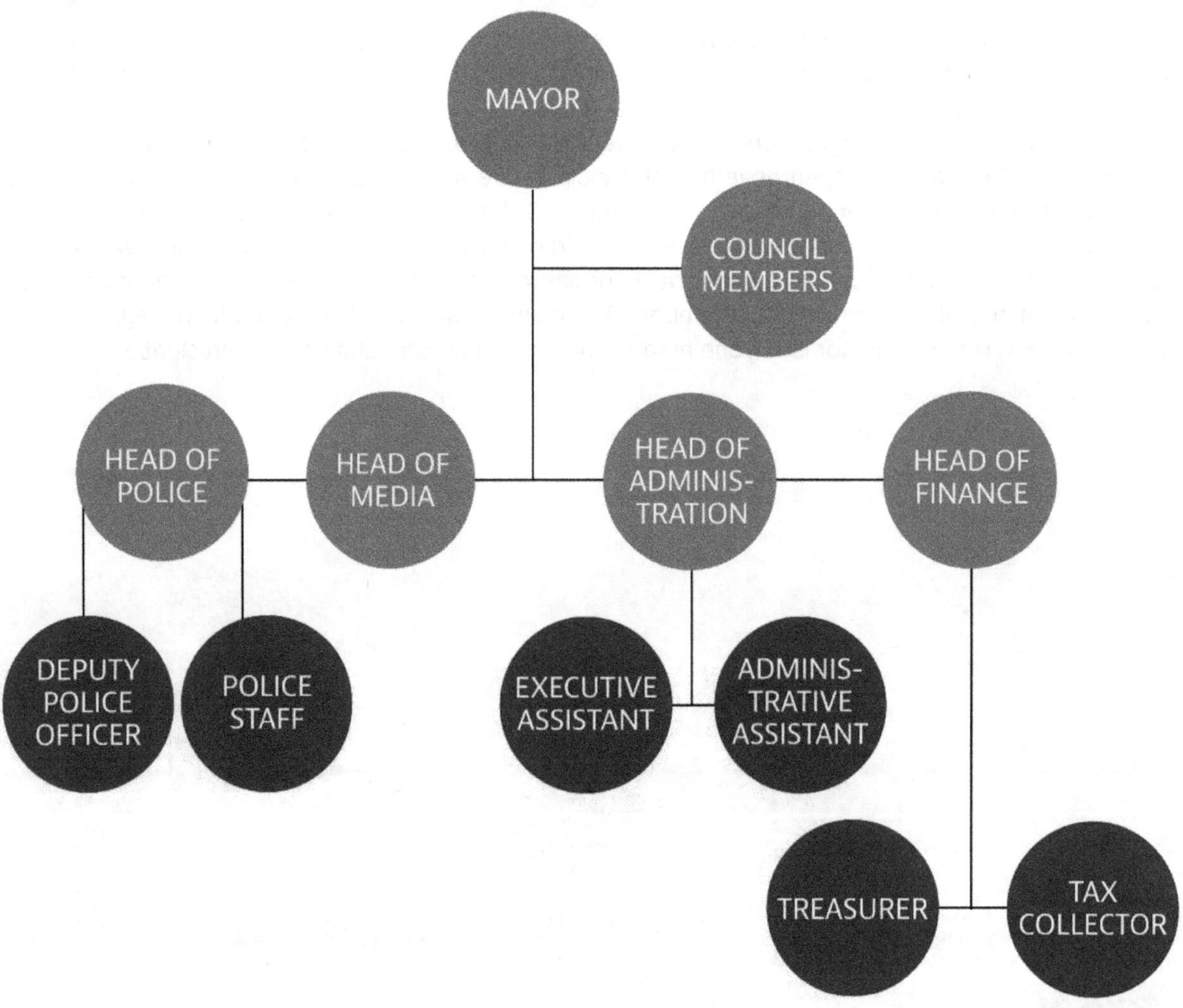

Source: Shweir Municipality, May 2019.

In some OECD municipalities there is an office responsible for participation that co-ordinates all participation initiatives, produces an overarching document to define their characteristics, and provides incentives for public officials to organise activities and for citizens to participate in them (OECD, 2016[2]). Byblos could consider establishing such an office, or an open government office with slightly broader responsibilities, such as responding to ATI requests. For a small municipality the size of Shweir, an adapted proposal is for the municipality to outline the objectives, characteristics and principles of stakeholder participation in its open government strategy, specifying who is responsible for implementation and monitoring. This could ensure that open government responsibilities are part of the official tasks/terms of reference of specific roles within the administration.

The OECD survey asked the two municipalities whether they exchange with other municipalities about good open government practices and whether they co-ordinate or collaborate with other municipalities on open government issues. In both cases, Byblos and Shweir indicated that they do not yet collaborate with other Lebanese municipalities on these issues; however, interviews with key members of the two municipalities identified a desire to foster such an exchange. Establishing a network of municipalities for open government could enable Byblos, Shweir and other municipalities to learn about good practices and to potentially share resources for related initiatives. The Office of the Minister of State for Administrative Reform (OMSAR), as the national ministry taking the lead on the open government agenda, could help to foster the establishment and co-ordination of such a network.

Human and financial resources

The impact of open government strategies and initiatives equally depends on having well-trained human resources and sufficient funds (OECD, 2019[34]). As such, the OECD Recommendation on Open Government calls on governments to implement reforms by "providing public officials... with adequate human, financial and technical resources, while promoting a supportive organisational culture" (OECD, 2017[1]). For instance, good public communication requires the technical skills to use different channels and clear language, as well as a strategic understanding of how communication can be used to leverage stakeholder participation. Interacting with citizens requires negotiation or mediation skills. Implementing the 2017 Right of Access to Information Law requires training in what this law entails. Civil servants also need to be aware and informed about the benefits that having an open government strategy and related initiatives can bring.

Human resources

The OECD Recommendation on Public Service Leadership and Capability stresses the importance of skills to turn political visions into high-quality services that improve citizens' lives (OECD, 2019[34]). The OECD Report, "Skills for a High Performing Civil Service", introduced a new framework for the skills that civil servants require today (OECD, 2017[33]). One of the four pillars identified in this report regards service delivery and citizen engagement, which are both particularly relevant for local government. The report summarises the skills needed as:

- **Professional**: Traditional building blocks of service and engagement skills including professionals with expertise in public relations, communications, marketing, consultation, facilitation, service delivery, conflict resolution, community development and outreach.
- **Strategic**: The use of engagement skills to achieve specific outcomes to inform, for example better targeted interventions, or nudge public behaviour towards desirable outcomes, such as healthier eating habits or smoking reduction.
- **Innovative**: The application of innovation skills to engagement in order to expand and redesign the tools themselves through, for example, co-creation, prototyping, social media, crowdsourcing, challenge prizes, ethnography, opinion research and data, branding, behavioural insights, digital service environments, and user data analytics.

Shweir municipality has taken a number of steps to provide training to all staff, not just those with responsibility for open government-related tasks, on transparency, integrity, emotional intelligence and interaction with citizens, as well as technical capacities to utilise the new information technology (IT) system. According to interviews with administrative staff, the aim of these capacity building activities has been to ensure the same quality of service delivery to everybody, without discrimination. OMSAR has also provided training to the municipality on implementing the Right of Access to Information Law. No such training has taken place in Byblos at the time of writing in early 2020, but this would be encouraged. Further training in both municipalities, in particular regarding the innovative skills listed above which are related to the implementation of open government initiatives, could also benefit the municipality's ability to involve citizens more closely in its decision making, projects, and public service design and delivery.

Financial resources

The OECD survey indicates that insufficient funding is one of the most significant challenges that both Byblos and Shweir face in implementing open government policies and initiatives. Respondents from Byblos also highlighted the lack of a clear separation of responsibilities between levels of governance, and respondents from Shweir acknowledged the lack of a requirement for open government reforms.

According to interviews with the president, mayor, council members and administrative staff in both municipalities, project funding from central government is not always predictable, and projects often stop part way through as a result. This is in line with the findings of numerous reports which highlight that transfers from the Independent Municipal Fund (IMF) are often late from one year to the next and are not delivered on a fixed schedule, meaning that municipalities often do not know when they will receive additional funds (Atallah, 2011[60]; Mourad and Piron, 2016[61]; Democracy Reporting International, 2018[63]; 2017[56]).

One third (35%) of Shweir municipality's budget comes from the national government through the IMF, while the remaining 65% comes from municipality taxes, which is a common funding structure in Lebanese municipalities (Mourad and Piron, 2016[61]). The municipality is responsible for the finances related to projects undertaken entirely by the municipality. When projects are co-ordinated by central government, however, the higher level is accountable, including for the procurement process. In these latter instances, central government informs the municipality, which plays a monitoring role. Interviews conducted underlined how these power-sharing arrangements limit the ability of municipalities to have full control over their open government policies regarding budget transparency and stakeholder involvement in budget decision making.

The municipality of Shweir also tries to implement open government principles through initiatives that are made possible by donations in kind. Interviews with council members conveyed that their proactive approach to seeking donations involves promoting a specific project, contacting well-off individuals and businesses in the community for their support, and, if donations are received, following their transparency procedures for disclosure. For instance, in response to such a call, a local cement company might donate concrete for a new building. The municipality follows an informal set of rules to ensure transparency with its citizens and the central government regarding donations. It provides a detailed description of the donation, involving its nature and its cost, on the municipality's website and its social media accounts, notably its Facebook page. However, this practice is not a legal requirement, and the municipality could consider embedding it as a provision in an open government strategy.

Shweir municipality also co-operates with CSOs and seeks citizen involvement to deliver some of its projects. Such an approach follows some trends underway in OECD countries to innovate public service delivery through co-production, referring to the direct involvement of individual users and citizens in public service planning and delivery (OECD, 2011). For example, in 2017 when the municipality wanted to establish a centralised low-cost medical assistance centre in Shweir, it established a public-civil partnership with CSOs and involved citizens in co-delivery. After asking and being granted permission from the Ministry of Health, the municipality established a new primary health clinic with the support of two health-related CSOs and citizen volunteers. The municipality and CSOs financed the building maintenance and supplies, the CSOs are paying the salaries of two nurses, and six citizens who live in the municipality volunteer as doctors. Such a public-civil partnership for public service delivery demonstrates that Shweir already has some advanced participatory practices underway, which could be expanded to other areas of service provision within its competencies. They could also be an inspiration for Byblos and other municipalities.

Recommendations:

- **Co-create an open government strategy for Byblos and Shweir with relevant stakeholders.** The president or mayor and elected representatives could, together with citizens, CSOs and other relevant stakeholders, identify the priorities in the areas of transparency, integrity, accountability and stakeholder participation. Such a strategy could include a vision, objectives and initiatives to be undertaken, as well as a set of monitoring and evaluation metrics that could allow for an impact assessment. Developing an open government strategy could help to enshrine the municipality's current culture of openness, thus ensuring its sustainability. It would also help ensure that citizens and stakeholders share the same vision.
- **Foster exchange with other Lebanese municipalities for the exchange of good practice on open government efforts.** Establishing stronger links could help enable the spread of good open government practices and initiatives in Lebanon, as well as a sharing of resources. OMSAR could help establish and co-ordinate such a network.
- **Provide training and capacity building activities to strengthen the skills required to implement open government initiatives in both municipalities.** In Byblos, training for all staff, similar to the one already conducted in Shweir, would be encouraged to cover transparency, integrity, emotional intelligence and interaction with citizens, as well as technical capacities to ensure that all staff have the same capacities to the use the IT system and social media. Training in both municipalities to strengthen awareness and knowledge of how to implement the Right of Access to Information law would also be helpful. Capacity building activities for key staff responsible for open government activities could cover topics such as co-creation, prototyping, crowdsourcing, challenge prizes, ethnography, opinion research and data, audience insights, branding, behavioural insights, digital service environments, and user data analytics. Such training could enhance the scope and quality of open government initiatives in the municipalities.
- **In Byblos, assign responsibilities to an individual or office for the handling of ATI requests and for stakeholder and citizen participation.** There is currently no individual or office specifically responsible for these important open government functions. Given the size of the municipality one person would probably be sufficient. However, an individual or office with this responsibility would help to ensure that the municipality is implementing the ATI law and is conducting regular and meaningful stakeholder and citizen participation initiatives to inform its work. This would lead to better policies and strengthen the relationship between the municipality representatives and administration and its citizens.
- **Continue and expand the use of public-civic partnerships for the co-delivery of public services in Shweir, and consider doing so in Byblos.** The new low-cost health centre in Shweir, established with CSOs and run with the help of volunteer doctors, demonstrates the municipality's capacity to use innovative methods to deliver better and more inclusive public services. This approach could be extended to other areas of service provision and could serve as inspiration to Byblos and other municipalities.

Implementation frameworks

The second pillar of open government regards implementation frameworks, which are the ways in which open government principles are put into action. These entail: transparency and access to information policies, public communication strategies, stakeholder participation processes, and monitoring and evaluation systems.

Transparency and access to information policies

The right to access government information is important as a foundation for open government at the local level as well as at the central level. Articles 45, 55 and 76 of the Municipal Act (1977) enshrine the principle of transparency to some extent. This has been strengthened with the recently passed Right of Access to Information Law (2017), which also applies to municipalities. Even though these legal instruments are in place, Lebanese municipalities publish only 10% of information related to their budget decisions, and fewer than 12% of municipal unions have a favourable opinion of the Right of Access to Information Law, according to a 2017 survey by Democracy Reporting International.

In Byblos, budgets are published on the Baladyati app for residents and on the municipality's Facebook page. In Shweir, there is a long tradition of transparency in the municipality, where budgets have been publicly posted since at least 1982, when the current head of finance took the post. However, the budget in both municipalities is published in a PDF format, which creates difficulties for analysis. It is common practice in OECD countries to publish the budget in an open data format – for instance, as a downloadable Excel document. Provision 7 of the OECD Recommendation on Open Government specifies that the format should be "free of cost, available in an open and non-proprietary machine-readable format, easy to find, understand, use and reuse, and disseminated through a multi-channel approach, to be prioritised in consultation with stakeholders" (OECD, 2017[1]). The majority of OECD countries (28) provide the approved budget and 24 provide the executive budget proposal at the national level in an open data format (OECD, 2019[40]). Byblos and Shweir could consider making the detailed budget more easily accessible and searchable for citizens and businesses by publishing it in an open data format.

Budget documents are often long and technically complex documents. By explaining and reporting budgets simply and clearly the government can enable better citizen and business understanding of the budget. In many OECD countries, governments publish a citizen's guide, sometimes called a citizen's budget, to explain the objective and impact of the budget in plain language. As of 2018, citizen's guides, in one form or another, are produced in 23 OECD countries (OECD, 2019[40]). According to the 2018 OECD Budget Practices and Procedures Survey results, they are most often published for the approved budget and the executive budget proposal (14 OECD countries for each). The Lebanese government also published a citizen's guide to the budget in 2018 and 2019 (Bissat, 2019[64]). To make the budget more accessible to its citizens and businesses, Shweir municipality could consider developing a citizen's guide to the approved budget. The OECD has developed relevant guidelines to help in this regard: "Producing a Citizens' Guide to the Budget: Why? What and How?" (Petrie and Shields, 2010[65]).

One example of what a citizen's guide looks like is the UK's 2018 budget, when the government published a simple breakdown of "24 things you need to know" (GOV.UK, 2018[66]). Each year when UK residents submit their tax returns, they also receive a table and a graphical pie chart breakdown of how their tax money was spent. Every resident receives this automatically. At the local level, the city of Brussels publishes a visual guide to the annual budget every year, which could serve as inspiration for Shweir on how to strengthen their budget transparency practices (Ville de Bruxelles, 2019[67]).

Another important open government practice in Shweir, in place since 2010, is the publication of the council's minutes of decisions on the municipality building, website and Facebook page. The latter has allowed the sharing of information to become more interactive, as citizens have asked about the rationale for certain council decisions on the platform, thus allowing for initial dialogue. This information is not published in Byblos at the time of writing in early 2020.

In both municipalities, the council publishes information about ongoing projects in the municipality and their status of completion, as well as the municipal plans and strategy. To ensure that this practice continues, municipalities could embed the approach to publishing information about projects, and subsequently about how citizens can participate in or offer feedback/complaints about council decisions, into their respective open government strategies.

In Shweir, where there is a specific person in the administration responsible for ATI requests, the municipality has responded to such requests in a timely manner. As discussed in the previous section, Byblos could assign responsibilities for ATI to an individual or office in the municipality to ensure that such requests are promptly handled and responded to.

Finally, procurement transparency is a key element of an open government agenda. According to interviews with council and civil society members, the procurement process in Shweir is considered transparent. For small local projects costing below USD 5 000, the municipality contacts two to three contractors who are required to bid, although this information is not published. Above this amount there is an open bidding process required by law. A tender is distributed on the municipality's webpage and on the front of the municipality building and is open for 30 days. The public can attend the town hall on the day the bids are opened and discussed by the mayor and the council. The municipality chooses the lowest bid that still meets the required technical evaluation of the project.

Public communication strategies

The OECD Recommendation (OECD, 2017[1]) identifies strategic public communication as a key pillar of an open government agenda that can promote transparency, enable participation and ensure accountability. However, fewer than 2% of commitments included in Open Government Partnership (OGP) action plans across the world are related to media and communication (OECD, 2016[2]).

Byblos has appointed a head of press and media who is responsible for public communication efforts in the form of updating the municipality's website, managing relationships with traditional media (TV, radio and newspapers), managing the municipality's Facebook activity and covering events. There is daily activity on Facebook and the head of media is promoting two-way communication by reacting and responding to citizens' comments on its posts.

In Shweir, the municipality is making strong and strategic use of communication campaigns and digital tools to promote open government principles and two-way communication with its citizens. Shweir's head of media is responsible for public communication efforts. Her responsibilities include updating the municipality's website and social media, covering events, and co-ordinating with key media (TV, radio and newspapers).

In both municipalities, public communication efforts could be strengthened through the development of a strategy for communicating open government initiatives. Existing good practices, such as awareness-raising campaigns and the publication of key information in bulletins and official documents, on the municipality's website, and on social media, are to be encouraged. Embedding these good practices into a public communication strategy as part of an overarching open government strategy could help ensure that they become systematic and that they support wider objectives.

Byblos and Shweir's Facebook pages are particularly active. The municipalities post updates about council decisions and social events, mostly with posts featuring photos or videos. Shweir also livestreams meetings.

The municipality of Shweir has shared some of its social media engagement metrics for analysis. These were not available for Byblos. As of February 2019, the average post reach per month is 98 000 views, the average post engagement is 68 000 and the average number of new page likes is 346 (Table 10.2). Facebook is an important communication channel given its prevalence in Lebanon. As of May 2019, Shweir municipality's page has 8 800 likes, which suggests that the municipality is also engaging a significant proportion of emigrants, visitors and diaspora, since the population is only 5 000 residents during the peak summer months and around 1 500 the rest of the year.

Table 10.2. Shweir Facebook insights

	Average per month
Post reach	98 000
Post engagements	68 000
New page likes	346

Source: Shweir Municipality, February 2019.

The municipality of Shweir has also began to engage on Twitter, although it only has 33 followers on this platform as of September 2019. However, this is unsurprising given the low penetration rate of Twitter (10%) compared to Facebook (78%) in Lebanon (Mideastmedia.org, 2020[46]). Shweir is equally active on Instagram, with 443 posts and 1 575 followers as of May 2019.

Beyond these measures of public communication, overarching objectives of what the councils would like to achieve through their communication could be set. The OECD guide on "Communicating Open Government" (OECD, 2019[68]) suggests establishing specific objectives that are SMART: specific, measurable, achievable, relevant and time-based. For example, an objective could be to encourage a cultural change in favour of open government principles. Key performance indicators for such an objective could include an increase in the number of citizens signing up for a particular participation initiative and an increase in the number of institutions using open data platforms. The guide also explains why and how to set targets and milestones, set responsibilities, identify audiences, and develop key messages.

Regarding other communication channels, Byblos's head of media is in charge of press releases and managing relationships with journalists from TV, radio and newspapers to ensure coverage. The municipality's website features a news section that highlights some of this coverage. Shweir's activity to engage traditional media sources is somewhat limited. Radio, TV and newspapers are not used to communicate about open government initiatives, which raises an important question regarding the digital divide. According to interviews with the municipality's head of media, there is a high level of certainty that the vast majority, if not all, of Shweir's residents are on Facebook and WhatsApp. Even if true, this does not necessarily mean that everybody is an active user of the platform. A diversified approach to public communication could help alleviate the potential digital divide and ensure that a wider audience is being reached and engaged.

In terms of other digital communication tools, Shweir could consider finalising the maintenance of its website and making use of it to proactively share relevant information. Byblos's website could be a source of inspiration. For both municipalities, another key outreach tool could be a citizen newsletter, which are an effective way of keeping residents up to date with municipality activities, projects and updates directly, reducing the need to seek out information. The city of Barcelona, for example, also offers its newsletter via the messaging app, Telegram, as more and more people use their mobile phones to find and receive information (see Box 10.4).

Box 10.4. Barcelona's citizen newsletter

The city of Barcelona invites its citizens to sign up for its regular newsletter, either via email or via Telegram. Below is an extract from the city's website:

"**Keep up to date with what's happening in Barcelona**

If you want to keep up to date with everything going on in the city you can get information of interest to you directly via e-mail.

All you need to do is fill in the following fields and you'll receive up-to-date content to match your preferences, whether relating [to] your district or to a specific topic. If your interests change you can unsubscribe easily using any of the mails you have received.

Got Telegram?

You can follow our Telegram channel to keep up to date with everything going on in Barcelona. Just type @bcnajuntament in the app or click on the following link t.me/bcnajuntament".

Source: City of Barcelona, (2020[69]), "Keep up to date with what's happening in Barcelona", http://e-bcn.cat/newsletter/en/landings/alta.

Stakeholder participation processes

As outlined in the OECD Recommendation (OECD, 2017[1]), the concept of participation refers to a scale of participatory practices that range from information to engagement, with citizens' involvement and influence increasing at each level (Figure 10.5).

Figure 10.5. Scale of participatory practices: Levels of stakeholder participation

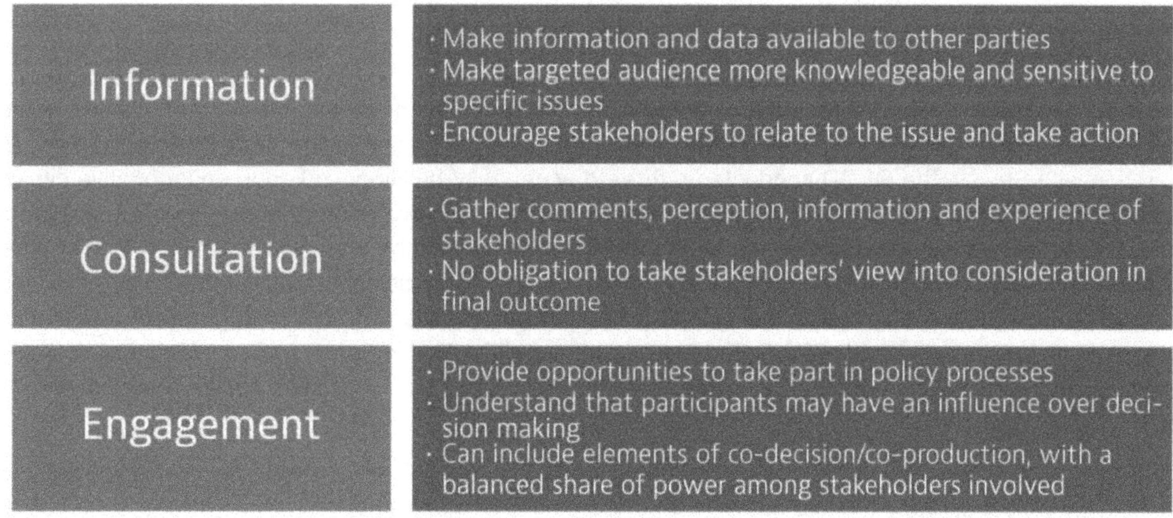

Source: OECD (2016[2]), *Open Government: The Global Context and the Way Forward*, https://dx.doi.org/10.1787/9789264268104-en.

Byblos and Shweir both have numerous examples of good practice regarding the first level of participation: information. The municipalities proactively share information and there is a two-way communication approach, as described in previous sections. The main element Byblos and Shweir could consider improving is access to municipal council sessions. Opening these sessions to the public is a common practice in the local authorities of OECD countries, and allows citizens and the press to follow municipal decisions closely (OECD, 2019[16]). However, in Lebanon, Article 35 of the Municipal Act (1977) stipulates that "Municipal Council sessions are held in secrecy". There is a potential way to overcome this challenge, as the same article also adds that "the President [Mayor] of the Municipality shall be entitled to convene any employee or person to the sessions of the Municipal Council and to listen to him". While the law prevents the councils from publishing minutes or broadcasting the sessions, it does allow the possibility of the mayor extending an invitation to all residents to attend the council meetings in person.

Regarding consultation, both municipalities also have numerous good practices in place, such as open door sessions and consultations for municipal, infrastructure and urban planning projects, both common practice in municipalities in OECD countries. To bring citizens closer to the council, in Byblos the president holds regular open door sessions, although the days and hours are not specified and this does not extend to councillors. In Shweir, the mayor holds open door sessions daily from 9am-12pm, and all councillors spend 2-3 hours daily at the municipality where they are open to meeting with citizens. According to interviews with the president, mayor, councillors and citizens in both municipalities, residents stop by every day during this period to discuss a wide range of issues.

In Shweir, the council also engages with stakeholders through a combination of these open door sessions, town hall meetings and Facebook posts where citizens are able to post their feedback. The consultations are currently targeted at citizens and could also be expanded to include other actors such as civil society organisations (CSOs,) trade unions, private companies, media/journalists and minority groups, such as the sizeable Syrian immigrant community. Moreover, to demonstrate to stakeholders how their input informs council decisions or how they are being implemented, a feedback loop between citizens and the municipality could be established and enshrined in the open government strategy.

Byblos identified four challenges of implementing stakeholder and citizen participation initiatives through the OECD survey: insufficient funding, insufficient incentives for public officials to implement stakeholder participation initiatives, insufficient citizen interest to participate, and interested parties are not sufficiently informed about participation opportunities. These challenges shed some light on the municipality's limited stakeholder and citizen participation initiatives thus far, which have been largely limited to information sharing and one-way consultations, without attempts at more innovative approaches or two-way engagement.

In Shweir, two main challenges for stakeholder and citizen participation were identified: a lack of adequate information among staff about different participation processes, and insufficient funding. As part of its co-operation with Shweir, the OECD conducted a three-day capacity-building workshop on innovative citizen participation practices in May 2019, with a peer from Belgium and two experts in the field from Belgium and Poland. The workshop was attended by the mayor, members of the municipal council, administrative staff and civil society. This workshop provided an introduction to participation more broadly and focused in-depth on deliberative processes, therefore addressing the question of how to engage representative groups of citizens in a process of facilitated learning and deliberation in order to allow citizens to develop informed recommendations. Many other forms of stakeholder and citizen participation were not covered in depth.

A similar workshop will take place in the municipality of Byblos in 2020, which could help to encourage the municipality to identify how it could better incentivise councillors and public servants to use stakeholder and citizen participation practices to improve policies and strengthen the relationship with inhabitants.

Beyond this capacity building, both municipalities could benefit from training on different forms of stakeholder participation, such as participatory budgeting, which is particularly relevant at the local level. The Participatory Budgeting Project states that "Participatory budgeting (PB) is a democratic process in which community members decide how to spend part of a public budget. It gives people real power over real money." (Participatory Budgeting Project, 2020[70]). PB started in Porto Alegre, Brazil, in 1989 and has since spread to 3 000 cities across the world (Participatory Budgeting Project, 2020[70]). It is a method that allows citizens to practice democracy and counter corruption as it introduces checks and monitoring by citizens. A 2019 World Bank study has also found that participatory budgeting and participatory institutions can improve governments' balance sheets as they increase citizens' willingness to pay taxes (Peixoto, Touchton and Wampler, 2019[71]). While PB practices vary across the world in their specifics, they usually follow a certain set of steps, according to the Participatory Budgeting Project:

1. **Process design**: A steering committee that represents the community develops the rules and engagement plan.
2. **Brainstorm ideas**: Through meetings and online tools, residents share and discuss ideas for projects.
3. **Develop proposals**: Volunteer "budget delegates" develop the ideas into feasible proposals.
4. **Vote**: Residents vote on the proposals that most service the community's needs.
5. **Fund winning projects**: The government or institution funds and implements the winning ideas." (Participatory Budgeting Project, 2020[70])

Byblos and Shweir could benefit from learning more in-depth about participatory budgeting processes through a training programme adapted for PB in small municipalities. However, as outlined in the previous section, with only a small proportion of the municipality's budget being raised directly through taxes, and the unreliability of funding from the national level, participatory budgeting might be a more salient option if the currently debated Decentralisation Bill becomes law, granting municipalities greater autonomy over their finances. This bill could also help contribute to resolving the issue of insufficient funding for stakeholder participation.

To address the challenges that the municipalities face, developing a participation charter that enshrines the principles, objectives and procedures for citizen participation in Byblos and Shweir could help to ensure that these practices are embedded. This charter could also establish a procedure for systematically providing feedback to participants in consultations. It is common practice in OECD countries to co-create this charter with citizens, civil society and stakeholders. As there is no legal requirement in Lebanon for the government, at any level, to consult or engage citizens in its policy making and decision making, creating such a charter could be one way of putting such a commitment in place, inspiring other municipalities to follow suit. For example, the Charter of Lyon helps to establish a common set of principles, objectives and a vision, setting out the rights and obligations of the municipality and citizens (Box 10.5).

Box 10.5. Example of a charter of participation

Lyon Charter of Participation

Greater Lyon established a Charter of Participation in 2003, setting out the city's principles, objectives, actors, direction, commitments, pilot projects, and monitoring and evaluation efforts.

Principles

- **Purpose**: Developing a more participatory democracy is at the heart of a strategy of sustainable development and the development of a strong culture. The charter aims to renew local democracy, strengthen the legitimacy of elected representatives, develop social links, restore public debate, facilitate free speech, encourage the expression of the voiceless and adapt politics to social demands.
- **Efficiency**: Consultation should allow for a better understanding of public actions, thus enriching projects and facilitating their implementation and ownership.
- **Subsidiarity**: For consultation on projects of local interest, the principle of subsidiarity will be privileged.
- **Adaptability**: There is no "one size fits all" method of consultation. It will therefore be essential to adapt the consultation strategies according to projects, actors, territories, and regulatory, technical and financial constraints. Exchanging experiences will allow for the construction of a consultation architecture.
- **Progressivity**: The charter does not set out a set of fixed and rigid procedures, but is part of a progressive, flexible and open process. It is part of a permanent and sustainable process. Local democracy is being built thanks to its progress and successes, but also with the experience of failures and frustrations.

Source: Grand Lyon (2003[72]), *Charte de la Participation*, http://www.adels.org/ressources/chartes/grand_lyon_charte_participation.pdf.

The third level of stakeholder participation, engagement, could also be strengthened in both municipalities. Consultations as currently carried out contain no obligation to inform citizens of the final outcome and tend to be top-down. Opening greater opportunities for citizens to influence decision making through methods of co-production and co-decision, where there is a balanced sharing of power between decision makers and stakeholders, could improve the quality of input that the municipalities receive from stakeholders and ensure that information comes from a wide range of socio-economic backgrounds.

This could be in the form of creating opportunities for everyday people in the municipalities to be able to provide informed recommendations on policy issues and projects. Deliberative processes are particularly well-suited for achieving this goal as they are designed to take a representative group of people, provide them with the time and resources to become informed and weigh all sides of an issue, and to develop concrete recommendations within the constraints of what is feasible for the public authority (OECD, 2020[73]; Chwalisz, 2017[74]; Gerwin, 2018[75]) (Box 10.6). However, deliberative processes are not the only option, participatory budgeting, mentioned earlier in this section, is also an example of such engagement.

Box 10.6. Example of deliberative processes for involving citizens more directly in public decision making

Gdansk: Three citizen panels about flood mitigation, air pollution and civic engagement

Since July 2016, the City of Gdansk has commissioned three deliberative citizen panels to provide binding recommendations on important issues such as how to prevent flooding, how to improve the city's air quality and how to make the city more inclusive, the latter focusing on civic engagement and the treatment of LGBT people. The participants in each assembly – around 60 people each time – were randomly selected through a lottery process, stratified to be representative of the city in terms of demographics and geography.

Each assembly met for at least four to six weekend days, spread out over numerous weeks, to have the time to learn, hear from experts, read all the relevant information, speak to their fellow family members, friends and colleagues, and have the time to deliberate with one another before developing recommendations. Stakeholders, CSOs and institutions were invited to present their positions to the panel.

Examples of the questions the panel contemplated about flood prevention include:

- What to do to improve rainwater retention in the Tricity Landscape Park?
- How should the city support the residents affected by a heavy rainfall?
- When building a new reservoir, should we give up filling it partially with water?

All proposals that received at least 80% of support from participants became official recommendations of the panels, which the mayor is implementing. Each panel has cost approximately EUR 30 000.

According to Marcin Gerwin, the main organiser of the citizens' panels, the key ingredients for success are a well-designed process, trust in people, inviting the best possible experts on the topic, and a willingness to implement the recommendations.

Source: City of Gdansk (2016[76]), "Civic Panel. Residents Decide", https://medium.com/@gdansk/civic-panel-residents-decide-e844590e88ec; Gazivoda (2017[77]), "Solutions: How the Poles Are Making Democracy Work Again in Gdansk", https://guests.blogactiv.eu/2017/11/20/solutions-how-the-poles-are-making-democracy-work-again-in-gdansk/; Gerwin (2018[78]), *Designing the Process of Delivering Recommendations by the Citizens' Assembly*, https://urbact.eu/sites/default/files/delivering_recommendations_-attachment_to_gdansk_case.pdf.

Monitoring and evaluation systems

The final key aspect of open government implementing frameworks are monitoring and evaluation (M&E) systems. These are essential for elaborating sound and robust public policies, ensuring that they achieve their intended goals and objectives, helping to identify the challenges involved, and providing possible solutions to overcome them. Provision 5 of the OECD Recommendation outlines three aspects needed to develop and implement monitoring, evaluation and learning mechanisms for open government strategies and initiatives:

1. "Identifying institutional actors to be in charge of collecting and disseminating up-to-date and reliable information and data in an open format.
2. Developing comparable indicators to measure processes, outputs, outcomes and impact in collaboration with stakeholders.

3. Fostering a culture of monitoring, evaluation and learning among public officials by increasing their capacity to regularly conduct exercises for these purposes in collaboration with relevant stakeholders." (OECD, 2017[1])

Monitoring and evaluation are complementary, although they are two distinct practices with diverse dynamics and goals. Policy monitoring refers to a continuous procedure of systematic data collection on specific indicators that allows policy makers and stakeholders to have access to information regarding the process and achievements of ongoing policy initiatives and/or the use of allocated finances (OECD, 2016[2]). Monitoring is important for planning and operational decision making as it provides evidence for performance management and can help identify implementation problems, delays or bottlenecks. It can also contribute to strengthening accountability regarding the use of resources, the outputs of a given policy initiative, or the efficiency and effectiveness of internal management processes (OECD, 2017[1]).

Policy evaluation refers to the structured and independent assessment of the design, implementation and/or results of a completed, ongoing or future policy initiative. The objective is to define the relevance and completion of policy goals and to assess various dimensions of a specific policy, such as its efficiency, effectiveness, impact or sustainability (OECD, 2016[2]). Evaluation serves three main purposes: 1) it allows policy makers to learn and understand why and how a policy was successful or not; 2) it allows for strategic decision making by illuminating the links between decisions and outcomes; and 3) it promotes accountability as it provides stakeholders with information regarding whether or not the government's efforts are leading to expected results (OECD, 2017[1]). At the national level, 86% of OECD countries monitor and 59% evaluate open government initiatives (OECD, 2017[79]).

M&E systems could be established for each of the implementing frameworks outlined in this section. This would require the municipality to identify an institutional actor or individual in the administration responsible for collecting and disseminating updated and reliable information in an open format. It would also necessitate the development of comparable indicators to measure processes, outputs, outcomes and impact in collaboration with stakeholders. For these recommendations to be successful, it is crucial to foster a culture of monitoring, evaluation and learning among public officials. Once ongoing monitoring is in place, the municipality could consider an evaluation of its open government initiatives to assess how open government improves policy outcomes and impacts.

For instance, measuring the extent to which citizens use their rights to access information could be one way of keeping track of transparency. An example of how this is implemented elsewhere is in the Australian state of New South Wales (Box 10.7). Measuring the number of access to information requests, waiting time and response given is one example of how implementation of the Right of Access to Information Law can be monitored and evaluated, although a high number of requests does not necessarily mean that there is a great deal of transparency, nor does having few requests mean that information is being made available proactively.

Box 10.7. Example of freedom of information monitoring

New South Wales dashboard

In the Australian state of New South Wales, metrics regarding the utilisation of information access rights have been monitored since 2014. The dashboard is a visual representation of the data, making it possible to easily track progress over time. The dashboard includes the following measures:

- Count of formal applications by type of applicant.
- Formal applications received per capita.
- Percentage of decisions on formal applications where access was granted in full or part.
- Percentage of all decisions made on formal applications where access was refused in full.
- Percentage of all decisions made within the statutory timeframes.
- Percentage of applications received which are reviewed by the jurisdiction's information commissioner/ombudsman.

Source: New South Wales Information and Privacy Commission (2018[80]), "Release of inaugural dashboard and metrics on the public's use of FOI laws", www.ipc.nsw.gov.au/news/release-inaugural-dashboard-and-metrics-publics-use-foi-laws.

Regarding communication, the municipality of Shweir is already measuring its social media engagement, which is a crucial element for understanding impact. This could also become a practice in Byblos. Both municipalities could also consider collecting more systematic data about their two-way communication to get a sense of what percentage of their communication is one-way information and what percentage is a two-way dialogue with citizens.

For stakeholder participation, collecting metrics regarding the number of participants and the level of input into a consultation, as well as the demographics of participants, could help the municipalities better understand which voices are being heard and not being heard, thus highlighting the potential need for targeted efforts to reach certain parts of the populations. This could also enable the municipalities to establish greater legitimacy for decisions taken, where a link can be drawn to the representativeness of the input received from citizens. Beyond monitoring the process, it is also important to monitor the outcomes and the impact of stakeholder participation initiatives on the desired goals, such as an improved policy or project, or increased trust in government.

Recommendations:

- **Publish the budget in open data format at the municipal level.** The Recommendation says that data could be published in a format that is "free of cost, available in an open and non-proprietary machine-readable format, easy to find, understand, use and reuse, and disseminated through a multi-channel approach, to be prioritised in consultation with stakeholders" (OECD, 2017[1]). In the case of the budget, each municipality could publish a downloadable Excel file that would allow citizens and businesses to easily search the budget and carry out calculations, as well as foster greater accountability of the municipality.
- **Create a citizen's guide to the budget that is automatically sent to all residents by e-mail and social media, and is available as a leaflet at the municipality.** Transforming the key elements of the budgets into graphical representations and explanations that are easy to understand by all people would help ensure the budget is more accessible to citizens, stakeholders and businesses. By sending it out automatically to residents by e-mail or social message (such as WhatsApp or Telegram, for example), the municipality would be proactively sharing information

rather than waiting for citizens to come to the municipality building or its website/Facebook page searching for information. To avoid a digital divide, and as not all citizens are necessarily active online, Byblos and Shweir could also consider making the citizens' guide to the budget available as a leaflet at the municipality building.

- **Incorporate a public communication strategy into the overarching open government strategy**. Evidence suggests that the current administrations in both municipalities communicate well about their respective open government initiatives and measure levels of engagement, but that these practices could be reinforced by a formal strategy. Including these practices in an open government strategy could help to systematise them.
- **Systematically publish information about local projects (e.g. indoor sports facility, the budget, etc.).** The practice for sharing information in both municipalities is currently ad hoc. The municipalities could develop a set of guidelines that ensure all information for every local project is always published on its website and social media pages, detailing which information needs to be shared with the public.
- **Extend communication beyond social media and develop audience insights.** The municipalities' use of social media to communicate, particularly on Facebook, is already excellent, generating high levels of engagement and two-way dialogue. Utilising other forms of communication in addition could widen the reach. Keeping the official website up to date is also important. Another method of communication, which is common in many OECD municipalities, is to develop a citizen newsletter that brings the municipality's news and information directly to citizens by e-mail or social messaging. In Shweir, adding a media strategy to increase TV, radio and newspaper audiences could help to ensure that the municipality is also reaching residents who are not active online. In both municipalities, developing analysis regarding audience insights could help the municipalities to better understand which types of residents they are reaching through which communication channels in order to develop a more targeted approach that could help Byblos and Shweir reach more people and increase stakeholder and citizen participation. Understanding audience motivations, perceptions and expectations are key for effective and strategic public communication.
- **Create a charter of openness and participation that includes guidelines for stakeholder and citizen participation.** As there are currently no guidelines, regulations or legislation mandating citizen participation and engagement in Lebanon, developing such a charter, which is common in OECD countries, could help to institutionalise the good practices already underway in Byblos and Shweir. The guidelines could set out the principles and objectives of involving citizens more in policy making and could establish methods of citizen participation. They could also ensure that monitoring and evaluation of citizen involvement occurs, keeping track of how many people participate in deliberations and consultations about each issue, as well as their representativeness of the wider community. The guidelines could outline indicators to help measure the outcomes and impact of stakeholder and citizen participation initiatives on policies and services.
- **Institutionalise stakeholder and citizen participation in infrastructure and urban planning projects.** To embed the municipalities' practice of holding open door sessions and meetings regarding infrastructure and urban planning projects, guidelines could be developed as part of a charter of openness and participation that could take these practices further, outlining in what instances they should be required, for example. If the municipalities choose not to develop a charter, then developing a set of guidelines for stakeholder and citizen participation that are enshrined in the open government strategy would be useful and set an example for other municipalities.
- **Develop monitoring and evaluation guidelines for open government initiatives at the municipal level.** These guidelines could detail the monitoring and evaluation requirements set out in an open government strategy in each municipality. They could identify the institutional actor or

individual within the municipality responsible for collecting and disseminating updated and reliable information and data in an open format. The guidelines could also entail the indicators that should be used to measure processes, outputs, outcomes and impact. For example, for stakeholder and citizen participation it could include monitoring the number of participants, their demographics and the feedback loop; and for transparency and access to information it could include metrics on access to information requests.

The way ahead

The way ahead refers to how the open government agenda can move beyond the frameworks, institutions and initiatives related to the enabling environment and implementation frameworks outlined in the previous two sections. It refers to public sector innovation, digital tools and open government data, and moving towards the notion of an "open state" (OECD, 2016[2]; 2017[1]). In Byblos and Shweir, there are already a number of initiatives heading in this direction. The municipalities have been proactive in disclosing information such as tax administration and budgets, as well as publishing council minutes (in Shweir) and other information digitally since 2002.

Both municipalities have a mobile application called Baladiyati, where citizens can access information, public services and submit complaints. In Shweir, a digital archiving system is under construction with the support of the Office of the Minister of State for Administrative Reform (OMSAR). A geographical information system (GIS) is also available, with 70 linked layers of data that allow for more analytical decision making regarding issues such as planning and new infrastructure. Furthermore, council resolutions are livestreamed on Facebook, and social media are used to communicate about social events, decisions taken and responses to citizens' complaints. Byblos could consider undertaking similar initiatives of digital archiving, establishing a GIS system, and livestreaming council resolutions on social media.

The next steps for both municipalities could be to consider how to incorporate more advanced consultation and engagement opportunities into the functionality of the app, or to use another application for these purposes. Some examples from OECD countries include the Government of Jersey's chatbot consultations with Apptivism, Barcelona's use of the free open-source participatory democracy platform Decidim, and Madrid's free open-source platform Consul. Consul has also demonstrated how online and deliberative forms of engagement can work well together, since the online platform has been complemented by a recently inaugurated Observatory of the City. The deliberative processes outlined in the previous section are also examples of more advanced engagement methods. The OECD report, "Innovative Citizen Participation and New Democratic Institutions: Catching the Deliberative Wave" (OECD, 2020[73]) covers this approach in more depth, analysing almost 300 case studies from around the world to better understand the principles of good practice and how such processes can be embedded into the policy cycle. Other examples of innovative citizen participation mechanisms can be viewed on the OECD's Toolkit and Case Study Navigator on Open Government (OECD, 2020[81]).

Box 10.8. Examples of innovative citizen participation mechanisms

Government of Jersey: Apptivism chatbots for more representative engagement

Between June 2017 and February 2018, the Government of Jersey ran six online consultations with a chatbot to assess public opinion. The chatbots simulate conversation with human users, so questions are asked in a more conversational way than via a traditional survey. Apptivism's co-founders describe their approach as "human-centred", applying the EAST (easy, attractive, social and timely) principles with both the citizens and the decision makers in mind. The topics included:

- Shaping our future: Environment and community on behalf of the Chief Minister's Department.
- Shaping our future: Community living in Jersey on behalf of the Chief Minister's Department.
- Review of maternity and paternity benefits on behalf of the Social Security Department.
- Review of the personal tax system, including the treatment of men and women, on behalf of the Income Tax Department.
- Survey on perceptions of the police and safety in the community on behalf of the States of Jersey Police.
- Review of divorce law on behalf of the Community and Constitutional Affairs Department.

Overview of key outcomes of the six chats

- 996 – average number of respondents per chat, uppermost among departmental consultations.
- 3 270 – unique users of Apptivism; instantly re-engaged each time a new chat was launched.
- 54.1% – percentage of users who "chatted" on more than one theme.
- 33 – average age of user.
- 57% – percentage of female respondents.
- 2 100 – qualitative free text responses received suggesting improvements to policies and services.

The Apptivism chats received more responses than most departmental consultations, while demanding less time from Government of Jersey officers. The chats received a comparable number of responses to previous surveys conducted by the Government of Jersey's statistics unit, but were not fully representative. Those without Facebook were not able to participate, although 87% of the population of Jersey is on Facebook, and this will not be a problem with future chats that will not require a Facebook interface. Men and those over 65 were slightly under-represented.

Re-engagement rates were high between consultations (54.1% of users completed more than one chat), and by using the same platform and approach there is a now a large user base (3 270 people) who can be easily re-engaged, which is not a feature of traditional paper or web-based survey consultations. In comparison, Mailchimp estimates that emails from governments and non-profit organisations receive a 2.76% clickthrough rate on average.

Apptivism engaged parts of the population typically under-represented by traditional consultation approaches, notably young people and women. The average age of respondents across the six chats was 33 and 57% of respondents were female. No socio-economic or ethnic origin data were asked of participants, however, so it is not possible to analyse whether or not the respondents were representative of the wider population in these respects.

Source: Government of Jersey, 2018; Apolitical (2018[82]), "With political apps, civic chatbots and digital forums, citizens are speaking out", https://apolitical.co/solution_article/political-apps-civic-chatbots-digital-forums-citizens-speaking/.

Government of Barcelona: Decidim platform for citizen participation

Decidim, which means "Let's decide now" in Catalan, is a free open-source software for participatory democracy, which has various spaces and tools for participation.

Spaces for participation

There are four spaces for participation where members are able to formulate their propositions and take decisions together: initiatives, processes, agoras and consultations. For example, there can be a citizen initiative to obtain a modification to a regulation (initiative); a participatory budget, vote or consultation to define a long-term objective (process); a general assembly of a workers' collective (agora); or a referendum on a specific topic (consultation).

Tools for participation

The platform also offers tools for participation, which are the functionalities that allow interaction between the platform and spaces of participation. Decidim proposes different tools: meetings, conferences, calls for ideas, proposition deposits, surveys and questionnaires, discussions and debates, results, project monitoring, votes, pages, and newsletters.

There are also three different types of participant on the platform: visitors, registered members and verified members. Visitors can see the content on the platform without registering, registered members can contribute to the platform, and verified members benefit from an extended level of participation, which comes with additional abilities to defend their propositions, sign petitions and vote in consultations. Individuals are able to register either as individuals or as members of an association or organisation. The developers consider Decidim to be more than an open-source platform, but instead a real community.

Source: Open Source Politics (2018[83]), "Comment fonctionne Decidim?", https://medium.com/open-source-politics/comment-fonctionne-decidim-da7f86805527.

Government of Madrid: Combining online and deliberative practices

A bottom-up, citizen-led initiative, Decide Madrid provides an open online platform for the generation and consideration of proposals developed by citizens. This process has drawn in everyday people, but has struggled to make their contributions substantive enough to work as hoped, and has not been able to bring their contributions to a public referendum when they were substantive.

The platform has experienced many problems common to other forms of "open" online participation. The loudest and most frequent voices dominate, the proposals do not draw from a wide variety of sources and are under-researched, leading to poorly informed recommendations. There is also the problem that it is hard to get the required number of signatures for any given proposal, meaning that it becomes more important to have the time and resources to run a good campaign.

To help counter this, the city council, with the help of Participa Lab and the newDemocracy Foundation, designed a citizens' council, which they have called the Observatory of the City, with 49 randomly selected residents. These people will meet eight times over the course of the year to learn about proposals in-depth, to deliberate about the trade-offs and to be able to come to a public judgement about the proposals. The council will be given the freedom to search through proposals on Decide Madrid and get further information to help improve or substantiate proposals that they choose to focus on.

The members of the citizens' council make a group decision to proceed to referendum. As the voter opens their ballot, they are informed by a report of a single page of pros and cons for each proposal, written by the citizens of the council as a trustworthy source to help them ultimately make their own considered decision.

Source: newDemocracy Foundation and ParticipaLab (2019[84]), *The City of Madrid's Citizen Council: Advice on Process Design*, www.medialab-prado.es/sites/default/files/multimedia/documentos/2019-03/Madrid-City-Council-%E2%80%93-Process-Advice.pdf.

OECD Open Government Case Study Platform and Toolkit Navigator

The OECD Open Government Case Study Platform and Toolkit Navigator features over 100 examples of innovative open government practices from OECD and non-member countries.

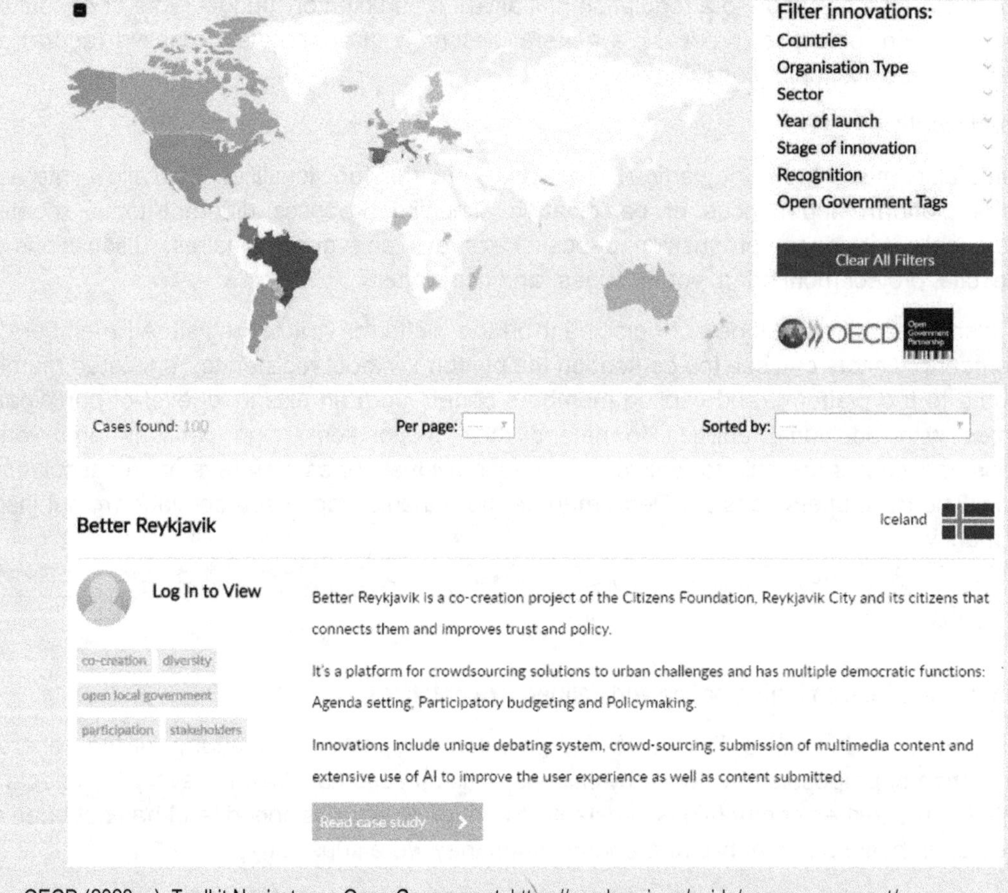

Source: OECD (2020[81]), Toolkit Navigator on Open Government, https://oecd-opsi.org/guide/open-government/.

Recommendations:

- **Introduce cutting-edge citizen participation practices that involve stakeholders more directly in public decision making.** The municipalities of Byblos and Shweir are currently undertaking good practices for information and consultation. The next steps to consider could be to implement more advanced citizen participation processes for engagement – which means involving stakeholders more directly as partners in policy making and public decision making. This could take the form of deliberative processes or advanced tools for online participation, for instance.

- **Expand the functionality of mobile apps to allow for greater citizen participation.** One way that Byblos and Shweir could implement the recommendation regarding cutting-edge citizen participation could be to expand the functionality of the mobile application to include the ability for citizens to participate in consultations (which is a two-way process), beyond the ability to submit complaints. Another option could be to utilise one of the free, open-source platforms available for this purpose online.
- **Continue the data archive process in co-ordination with OMSAR in Shweir, and begin it in Byblos, alongside the development of a GIS system.** The municipalities could ensure that data are in an open format which is easily downloadable, searchable and shareable, as per the OECD's Recommendation on Open Government (OECD, 2017[1]).
- **To support a broader open state agenda, consider creating a mechanism through which municipalities and OMSAR can collaborate and share good practices.** Such a mechanism can take the form of a mixed commission with representatives from all levels of government, including at both the local and national levels. Likewise, the group could horizontally convene both government and non-governmental stakeholders across ministries and sectors.

Notes

[1] Municipal unions are sometimes called municipal federations.

[2] The municipality of Beirut is an exception. The government-appointed Governor of Beirut chairs the executive authority and the mayor of Beirut is responsible for policy making alongside the councillors. From a legal perspective, Beirut's mayor has the same powers as the councillors, but in practice, he is also the leader and spokesperson of the elected council (Democracy Reporting International, 2017[56]).

[3] The Ta'if Agreement ended the civil war in Lebanon. It was negotiated in Ta'if, Saudi Arabia in September 1989 and approved by the Lebanese parliament on 4 November 1989. The full text is available here: www.un.int/lebanon/sites/www.un.int/files/Lebanon/the_taif_agreement_english_version_.pdf.

References

Apolitical (2018), *"With political apps, civic chatbots and digital forums, citizens are speaking out"*, Online article, https://apolitical.co/solution_article/political-apps-civic-chatbots-digital-forums-citizens-speaking/. [35]

Atallah, S. (2011), *The Independent Municipal Fund: Reforming the Distributional Criteria*, Lebanese Centre for Policy Studies, http://www.lcps-lebanon.org/publications/1331312295-imf-policybrief-eng.pdf. [8]

Bissat, L. (2019), *"Lebanon releases the 2019 citizen budget"*, Online article, Executive Magazine, https://www.executive-magazine.com/economics-policy/lebanon-releases-the-2019-citizen-budget. [16]

Chwalisz, C. (2017), *The People's Verdict: Adding Informed Citizen Voices in Public Decision-making*, Rowman & Littlefield, London, https://www.rowmaninternational.com/book/the_peoples_verdict/3-156-18082fd3-2549-4b20-9f33-a7c4a1c93027. [27]

City of Barcelona (2020), *"Keep up to date with what's happening in Barcelona" webpage*, http://e-bcn.cat/newsletter/en/landings/alta (accessed on 1 July 2020). [22]

City of Edmonton (2017), *Open City Initiative*, http://www.edmonton.ca/city_government/documents/Open_City_Initiative.pdf. [10]

City of Gdansk (2016), *"Civic Panel. Residents Decide"*, Online article, https://medium.com/@gdansk/civic-panel-residents-decide-e844590e88ec. [29]

Democracy Reporting International (2019), *Survey Results: Are Municipalities in Lebanon Delivering?*, https://democracy-reporting.org/dri_publications/are-municipalities-in-lebanon-delivering/. [6]

Democracy Reporting International (2018), *Local Governance in Lebanon: The Way Forward*, https://democracy-reporting.org/dri_publications/bp-93-local-governance-in-lebanon-the-way-forward/. [14]

Democracy Reporting International (2017), *Reforming Decentralisation in Lebanon: The State of Play*, https://democracy-reporting.org/dri_publications/bp-80-reforming-decentralisation-in-lebanon-the-state-of-play/. [4]

Gazivoda, T. (2017), *"Solutions: How the Poles Are Making Democracy Work Again in Gdansk"*, Online article, https://guests.blogactiv.eu/2017/11/20/solutions-how-the-poles-are-making-democracy-work-again-in-gdansk/. [30]

Gerwin, M. (2018), *Citizens' Assemblies: Guide to Democracy That Works*, Otwarty Plan, Kraków, https://citizensassemblies.org/wp-content/uploads/2018/10/Citizens-Assemblies_EN_web.pdf. [28]

Gerwin, M. (2018), *Designing the Process of Delivering Recommendations by the Citizens' Assembly*, Urbact EU, https://urbact.eu/sites/default/files/delivering_recommendations_-attachment_to_gdansk_case.pdf. [31]

GOV.UK (2018), *"Budget 2018: 24 things you need to know"*, Online article, https://www.gov.uk/government/news/budget-2018-24-things-you-need-to-know. [18]

Grand Lyon (2003), *Charte de la Participation*, http://www.adels.org/ressources/chartes/grand_lyon_charte_participation.pdf. [25]

Mideastmedia.org (2020), *"Social Media: Use by Platform" webpage*, http://www.mideastmedia.org/survey/2017/chapter/social-media/ (accessed on 2 July 2020). [20]

Mourad, L. and L. Piron (2016), *Municipal Service Delivery, Stability, Social Cohesion and Legitimacy in Lebanon: An Analytical Literature Review*, UK Department for International Development, https://www.semanticscholar.org/paper/Municipal-Service-Delivery%2C-Stability%2C-Social-and-Mourad-Piron/ea663c71b7bc530d5be35b69d29eabc7c4073a45#paper-header. [9]

New South Wales Information and Privacy Commission (2018), *"Release of inaugural dashboard and metrics on the public's use of FOI laws"*, Online article, https://www.ipc.nsw.gov.au/news/release-inaugural-dashboard-and-metrics-publics-use-foi-laws. [33]

newDemocracy Foundation and ParticipaLab (2019), *The City of Madrid's Citizen Council: Advice on Process Design*, https://www.medialab-prado.es/sites/default/files/multimedia/documentos/2019-03/Madrid-City-Council- [37]

%E2%80%93-Process-Advice.pdf.

OECD (2020), *Innovative Citizen Participation and New Democratic Institutions: Catching the Deliberative Wave*, OECD Publishing, Paris, https://dx.doi.org/10.1787/339306da-en. [26]

OECD (2020), *Toolkit Navigator on Open Government*, https://oecd-opsi.org/guide/open-government/ (accessed on 29 June 2020). [34]

OECD (2019), *Budgeting and Public Expenditures in OECD Countries 2019*, OECD Publishing, Paris, https://dx.doi.org/10.1787/9789264307957-en. [15]

OECD (2019), *Communicating Open Government: A How-To Guide*, OECD, Paris, https://www.oecd.org/gov/Open-Government-Guide.pdf. [21]

OECD (2019), *Open Government in Tunisia: La Marsa, Sayada and Sfax*, OECD Public Governance Reviews, OECD Publishing, Paris, https://dx.doi.org/10.1787/9789264310995-en. [11]

OECD (2019), *Recommendation of the Council on Public Service Leadership and Capability*, https://legalinstruments.oecd.org/en/instruments/OECD-LEGAL-0445 (accessed on 29 October 2019). [12]

OECD (2017), "Monitoring and evaluation of open government strategies", in *Government at a Glance 2017*, OECD Publishing, Paris, https://dx.doi.org/10.1787/gov_glance-2017-66-en. [32]

OECD (2017), *Recommendation of the Council on Open Government*, https://legalinstruments.oecd.org/en/instruments/OECD-LEGAL-0438. [1]

OECD (2017), *Recommendation of the Council on Public Integrity*, OECD, Paris, http://www.oecd.org/gov/ethics/OECD-Recommendation-Public-Integrity.pdf. [3]

OECD (2017), *Skills for a High Performing Civil Service*, OECD Public Governance Reviews, OECD Publishing, Paris, https://dx.doi.org/10.1787/9789264280724-en. [13]

OECD (2016), *Open Government: The Global Context and the Way Forward*, OECD Publishing, Paris, https://dx.doi.org/10.1787/9789264268104-en. [2]

OECD/UCLG (2016), *Subnational Governments Around the World: Structure and Finance.*, OECD, Paris, https://www.oecd.org/regional/regional-policy/Subnational-Governments-Around-the-World-%20Part-I.pdf. [7]

Open Source Politics (2018), *"Comment fonctionne Decidim?"*, Online article, https://medium.com/open-source-politics/comment-fonctionne-decidim-da7f86805527. [36]

Participatory Budgeting Project (2020), *"What is PB?" webpage*, https://www.participatorybudgeting.org/what-is-pb/ (accessed on 1 July 2020). [23]

Peixoto, T., M. Touchton and B. Wampler (2019), *Of Governance and Revenue: Participatory Institutions and Tax Compliance in Brazil*, Work Bank Group Governance World Practice, https://openknowledge.worldbank.org/bitstream/handle/10986/31492/WPS8797.pdf. [24]

Petrie, M. and J. Shields (2010), *Producing a Citizens' Guide to the Budget: Why, What and How?*, OECD Journal on Budgeting, Vol. 2., OECD, Paris, https://www.oecd.org/gov/budgeting/48170438.pdf. [17]

The Lebanese Center for Policy Studies (2015), *About Administrative Decentralization in Lebanon*, The Lebanese Center for Policy Studies, Beirut. [5]

Ville de Bruxelles (2019), *Dossier de Presse Budget 2019*, https://www.brussels.be/sites/default/files/bxl/budget_WEB_FR.pdf. [19]

www.ingramcontent.com/pod-product-compliance
Lightning Source LLC
LaVergne TN
LVHW081412110826
845149LV00010B/1723

* 9 7 8 9 2 6 4 3 6 5 9 8 8 *